I0559482

Dot Markers Activity Coloring Book for Kids 2-5

Numbers, ABC Letters, Shapes, Tracing & Cute Animals | Learning with Fun, Educational Pages to Boost Creativity and Fine Motor Skills | Interactive Alphabet for Toddlers & Preschoolers Boys and Girls

POLYMATH
Panda

ISBN: 978-1-953149-67-1

This Book Belongs To:

_____

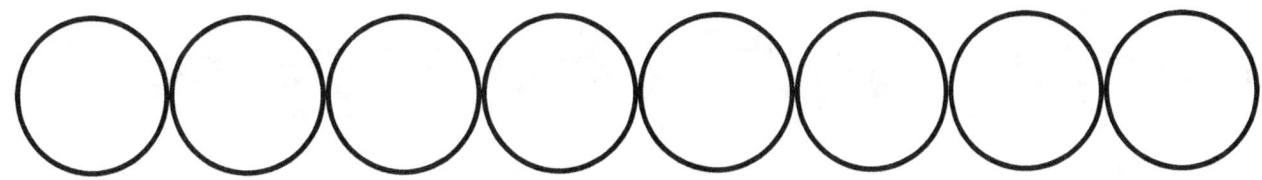

Grab Your Dot Markers and Dive into 50
Fun-Filled Pages of ABCs, 123s, Tracing and Shapes!

Featuring the complete A-Z alphabet, numbers from 0-10, and many first shapes... all designed with large, easy-to-color dots. Perfectly compatible with all leading dot marker brands with consistent 0.75 inch (18mm) dots.

This book is a fantastic fit for young explorers aged 2 - 5. It's crafted to enhance your child's early learning journey with delightful designs that connect letters, words, images, and colors. Our team of skilled designers has ensured each page stimulates your child's imagination and helps build their fine motor skills, making learning an exciting adventure!

We understand the enthusiasm of young dot marker artists, so we've designed each page to be single-sided, minimizing the risk of colors bleeding through. Additionally, placing a sheet of paper or card between the pages can be a great way to keep everything tidy!

Thank you for choosing this book! We hope it brings you and your child countless hours of dot marker joy and learning.

Free Printable Activity Book!

- **Enhances Creativity:** Fun dot marker coloring pages.
- **Builds Fine Motor Skills:** Scissor skill exercises and dot-to-dot puzzles.
- **Boosts Cognitive Development:** Simple addition with numbers and images.
- **Encourages Observation:** Engaging I Spy games.
- **Hours of Fun:** Full kawaii coloring pages designed for young children.

QR Code in the Back of the Book

Enjoying this Book?

We'd love to hear your thoughts

We may just send you something special.

SCAN ME

A a

Dot all the "A" and "a"

D

A a

A

B e c

a

ANT

L a

A

P J m

P A

A K p

O

A

Trace it

A A A a a a

Bb

Dot all the "B" and "b"

D q L
w i B a
p e a m B
J
h P
b b

BUTTERFLY

Trace it

B B B b b b

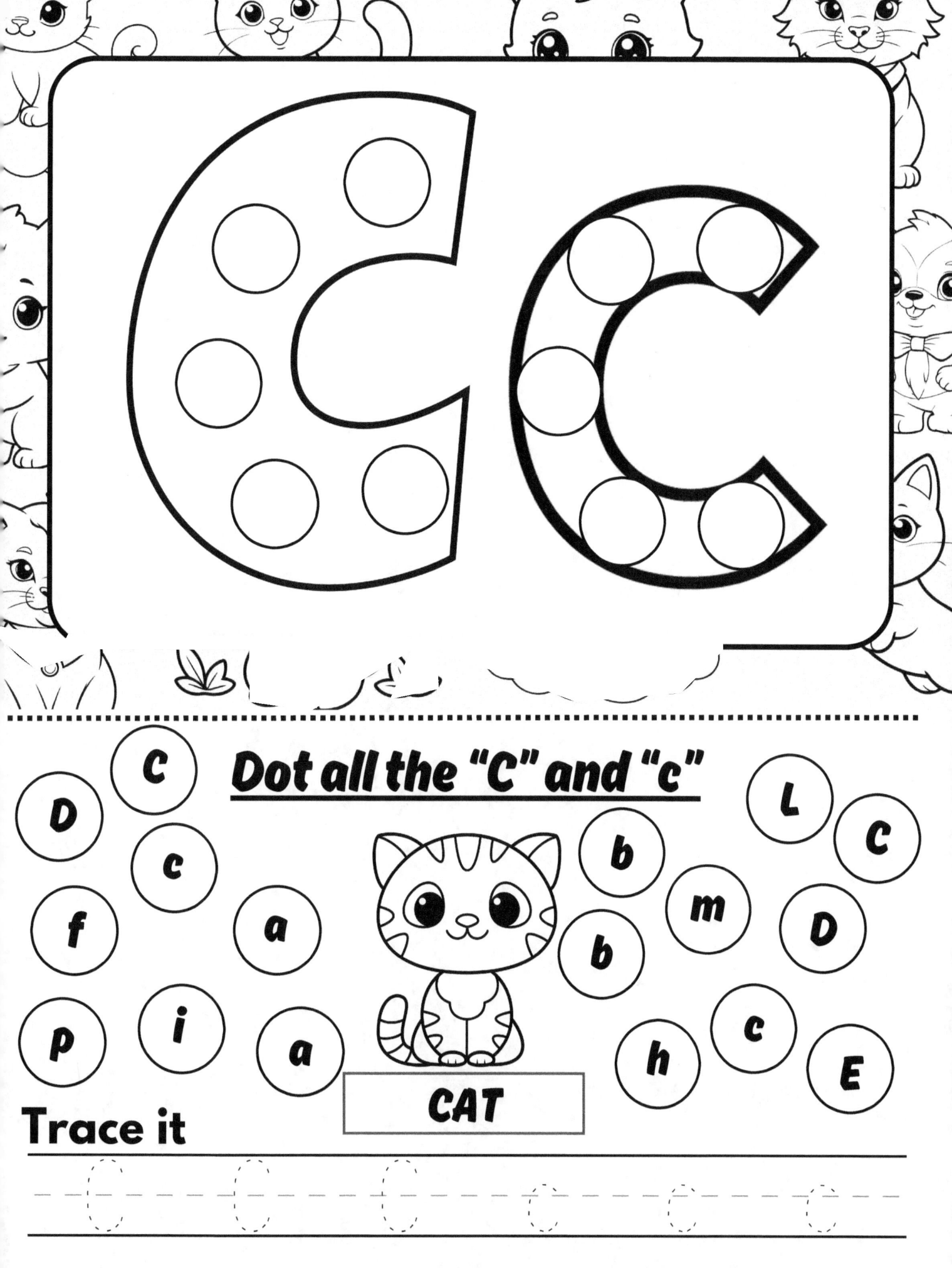

Cc

Dot all the "C" and "c"

D · c
c · D
f · a · b
p · i · a · m · D
b
L · C
h · c · E

CAT

Trace it

Dd

Dot all the "D" and "d"

D c P d

k d a b x D

P D a b E

Dolphin h d

Trace it

Dot all the "E" and "e"

Elephant

Trace it

Ff

Dot all the "F" and "f"

f j
z
E f
E L
D e

E i
F
b K
f M
b

Firefly

Trace it

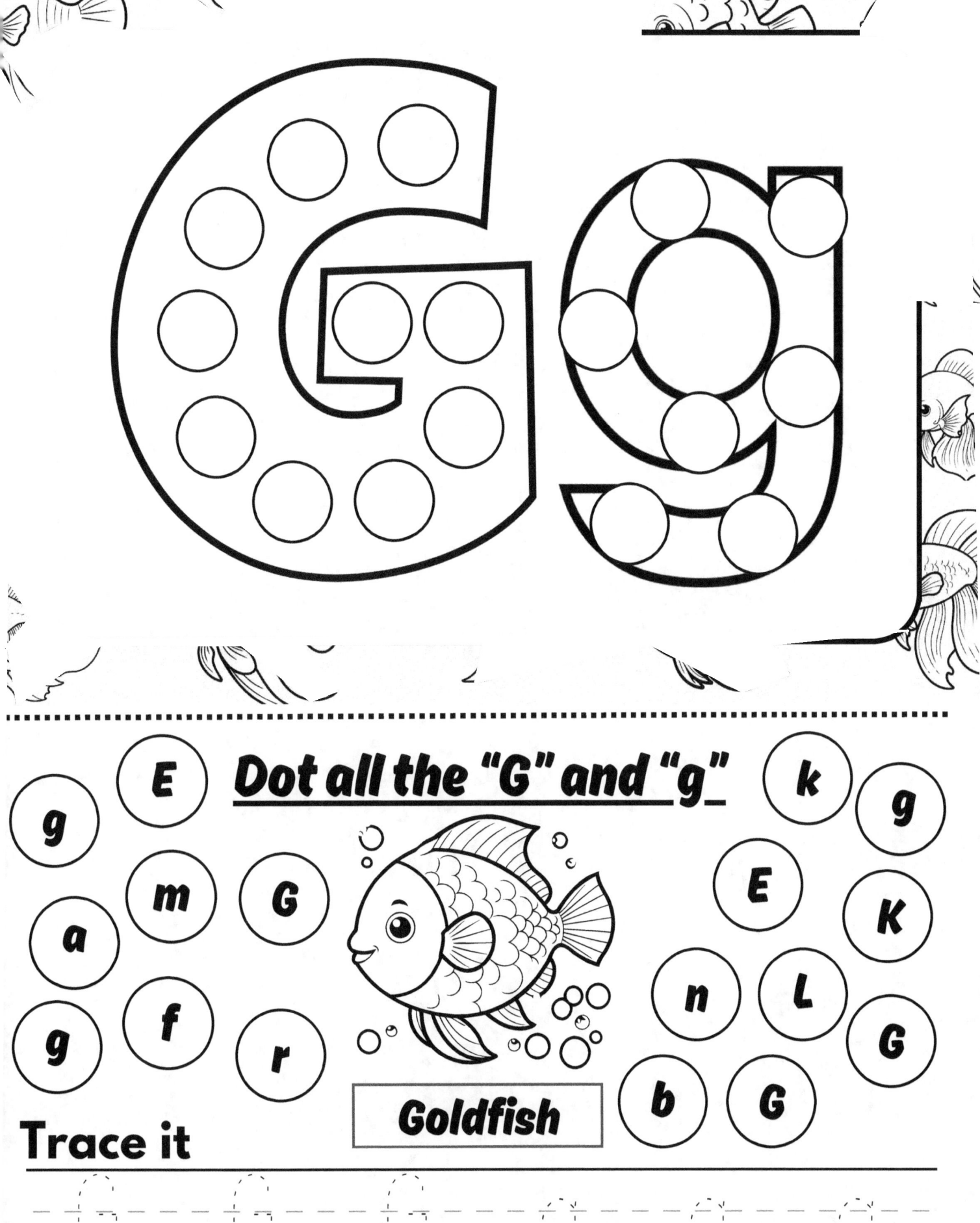

Dot all the "G" and "g"

g E a m G g f r

Goldfish

k g E K n L G b G

Trace it

H h

Dot all the "H" and "h"

O E g
f h k H E K
H f r b L
g n
m G
Hawk H

Trace it

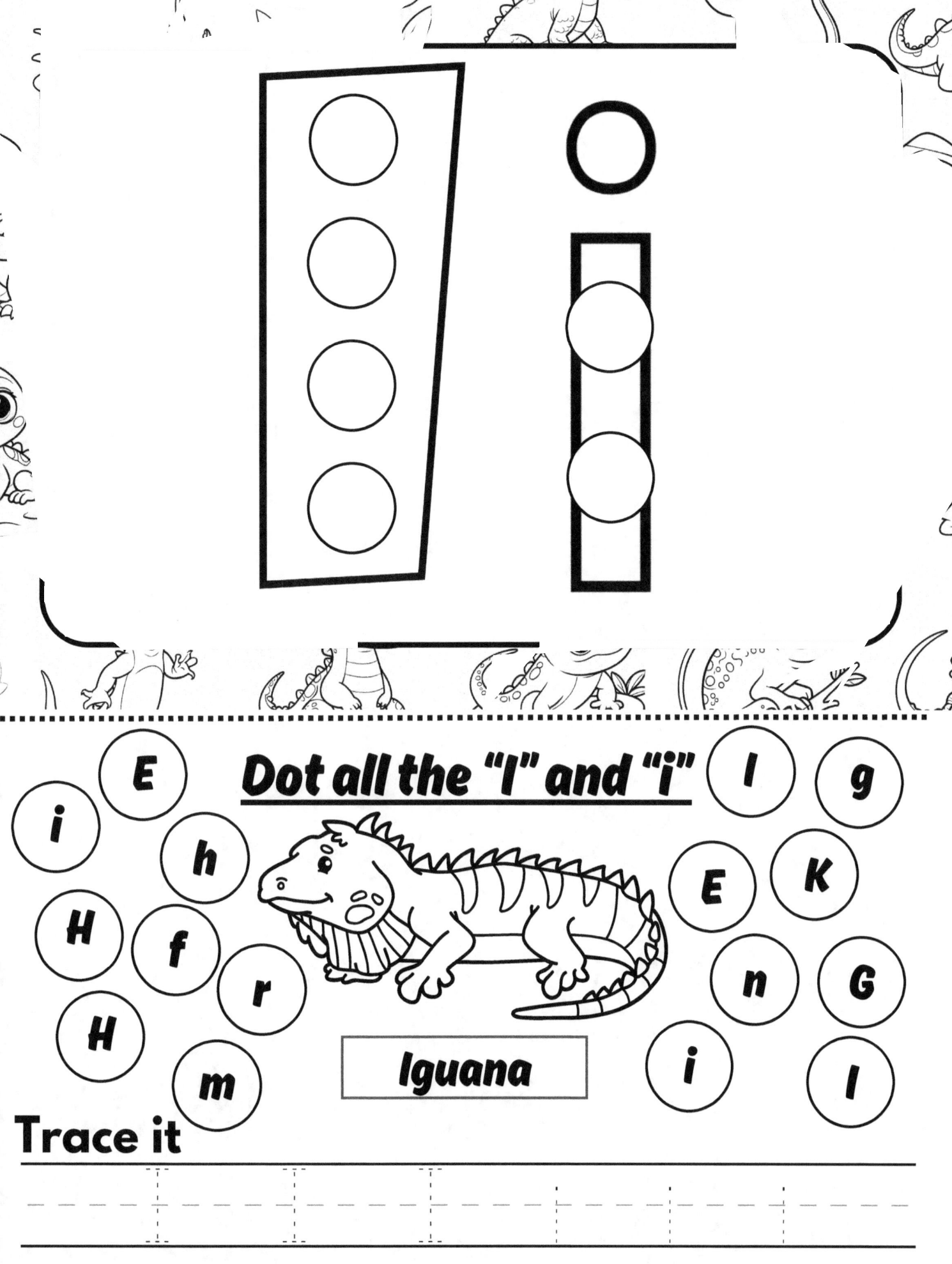

Dot all the "I" and "i"

Iguana

Trace it

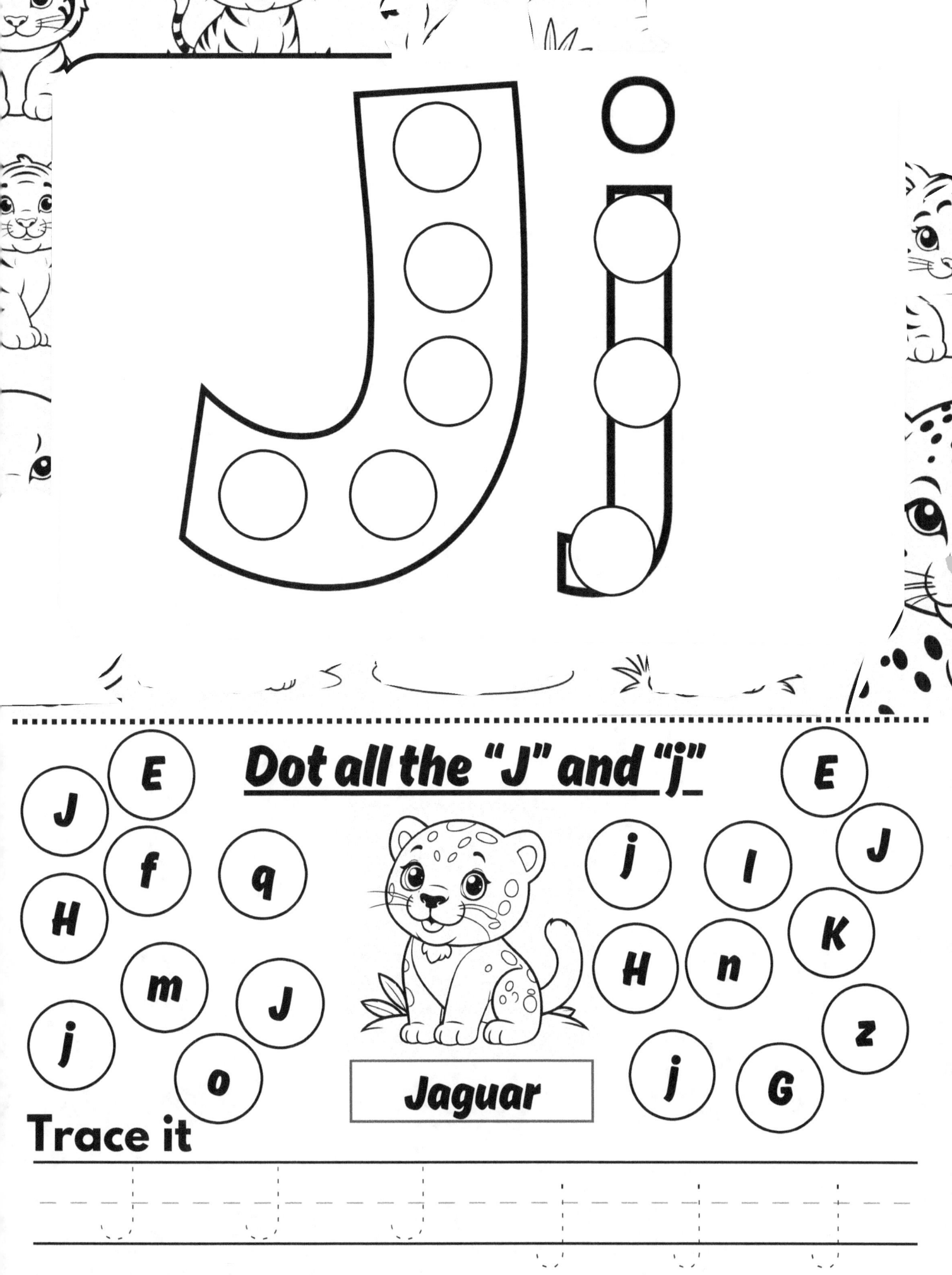

Dot all the "J" and "j"

Jaguar

Trace it

Dot all the "K" and "k"

Kangaroo

Trace it

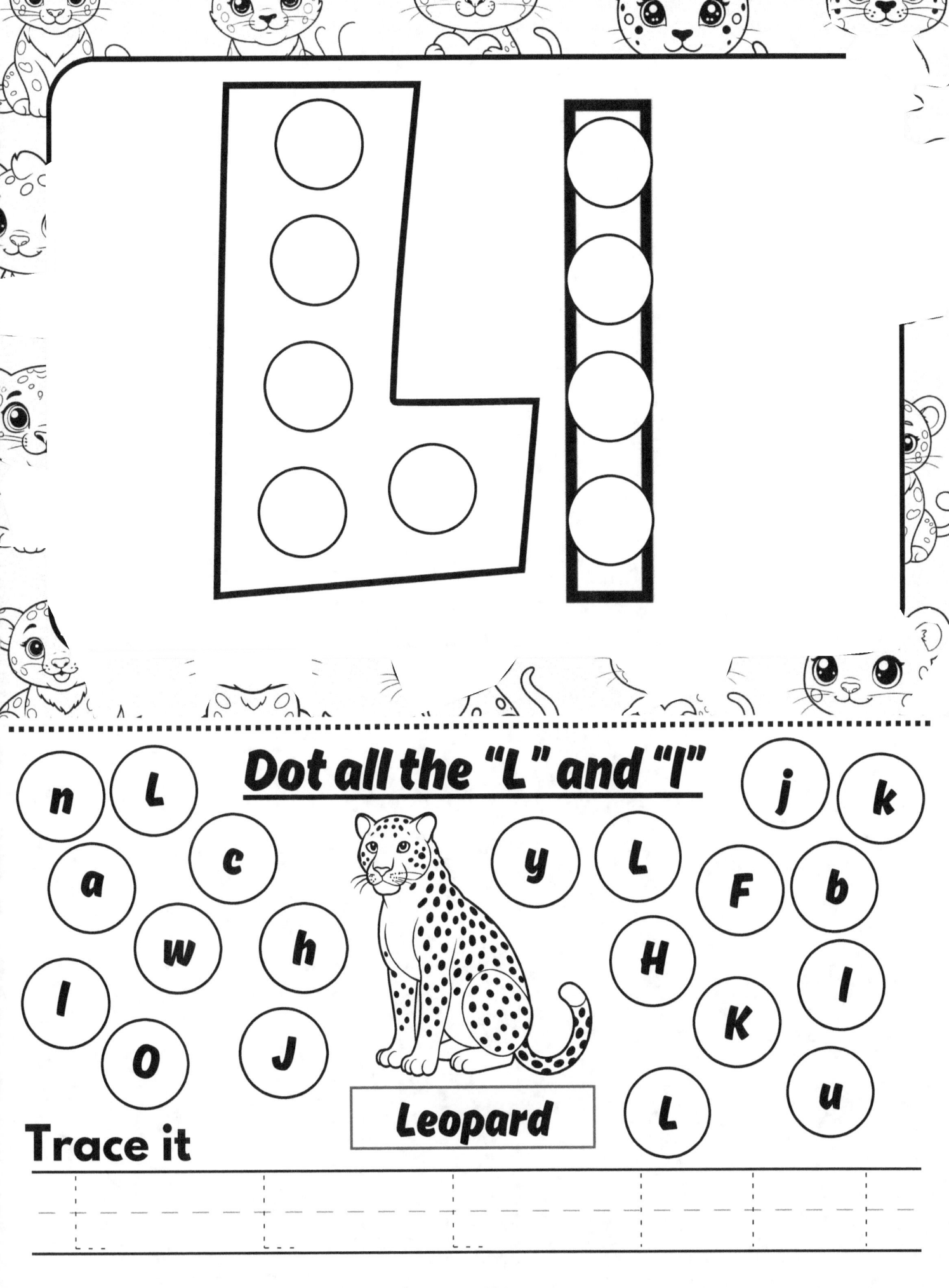

Dot all the "L" and "l"

Leopard

Trace it

Mm

Dot all the "M" and "m"

u K G

w s F r

J m M

O j k

t J m P

Moose

Trace it

M M M m m m

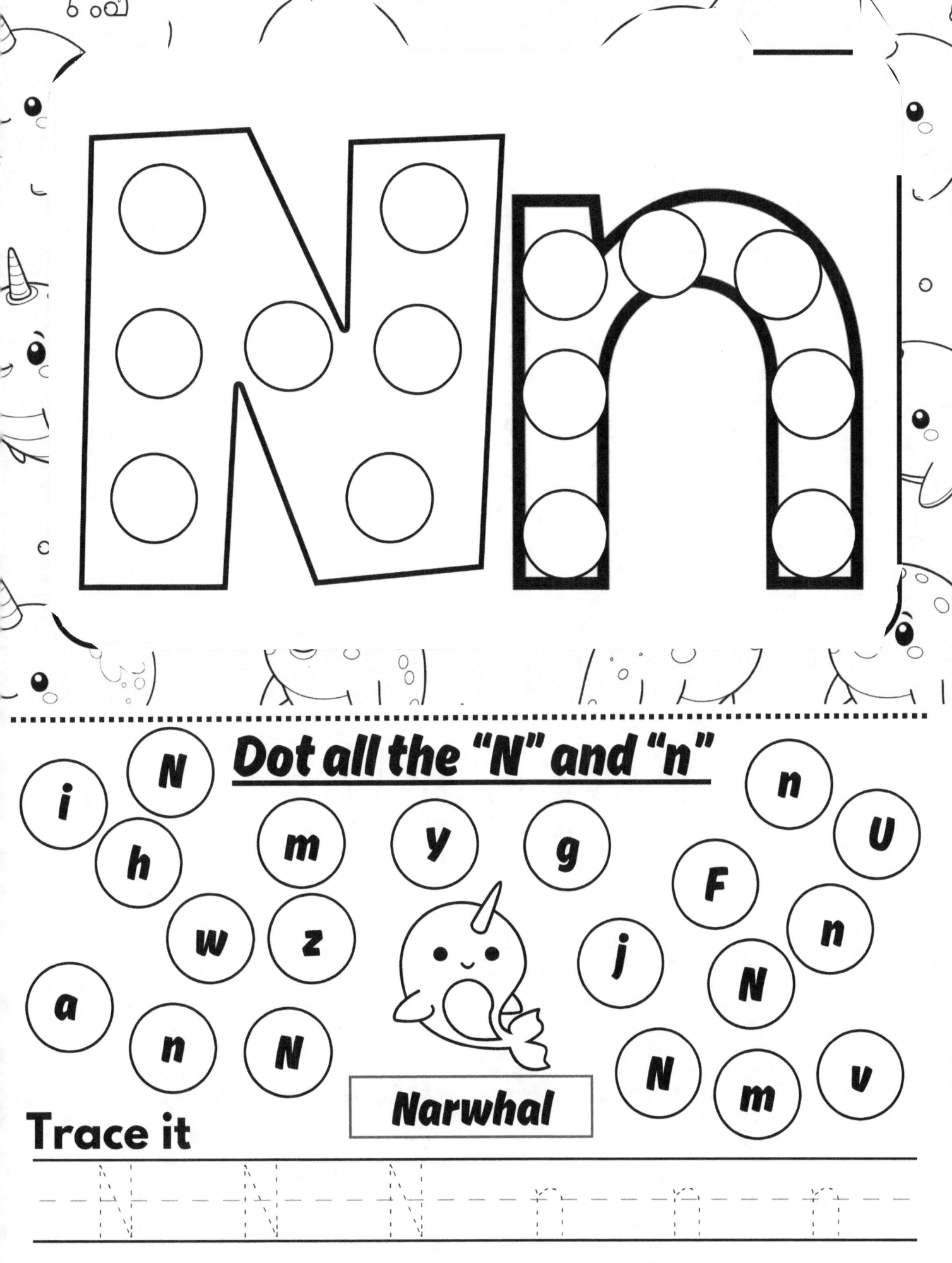

Dot all the "N" and "n"

Narwhal

Trace it

Dot all the "O" and "o"

Trace it

Octopus

P p

Dot all the "P" and "p"

h
r
n P
n
p
n
x

q
w
i

Panda

F P
O M
P M
S
N
P w

Trace it

P P P p p

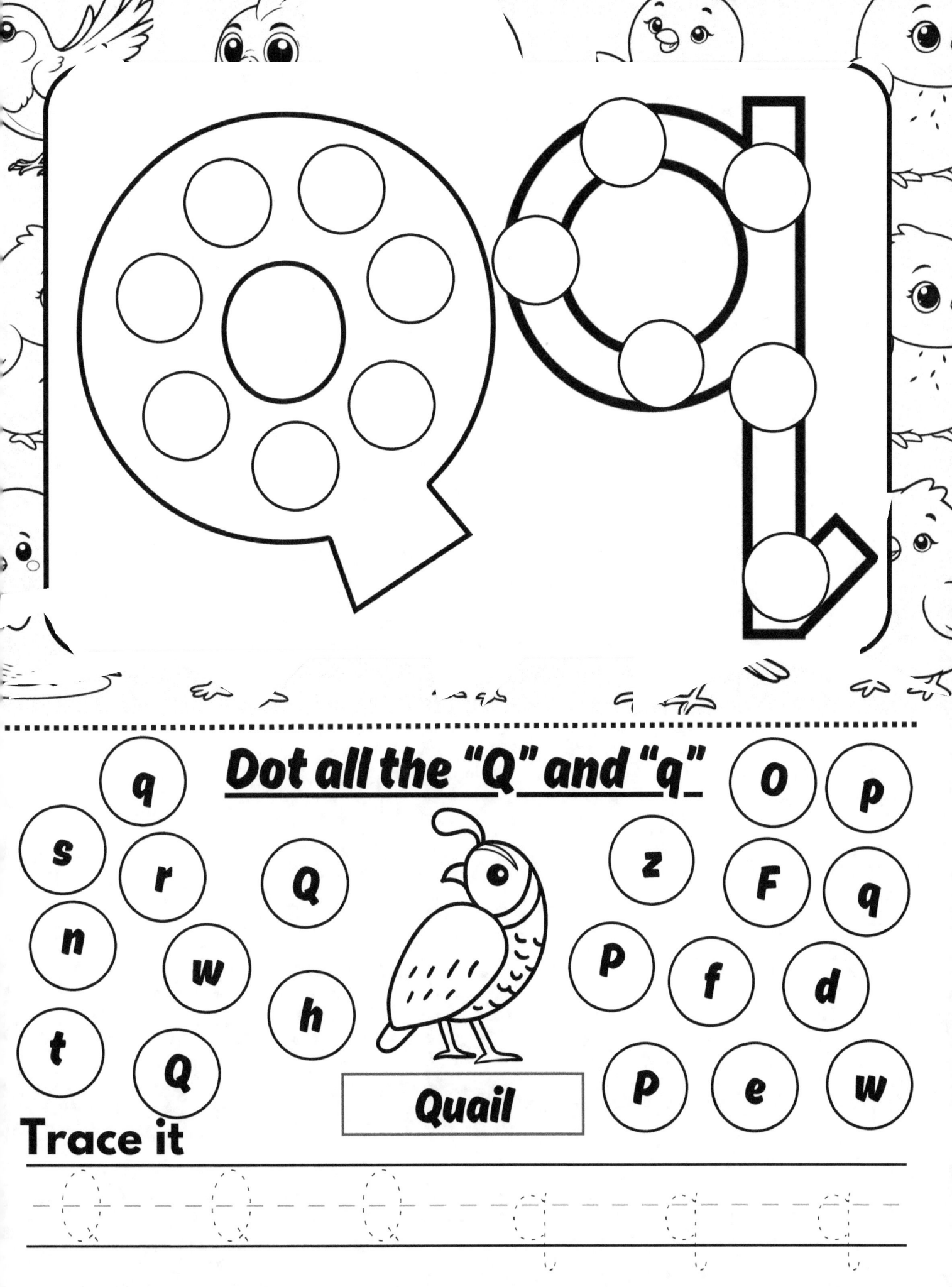

Dot all the "Q" and "q"

q
s
r
n
w
h
t
Q

Q

O   P
z
F   q
P   f   d
P   e   w

Quail

Trace it

Dot all the "R" and "r"

Trace it

Robin

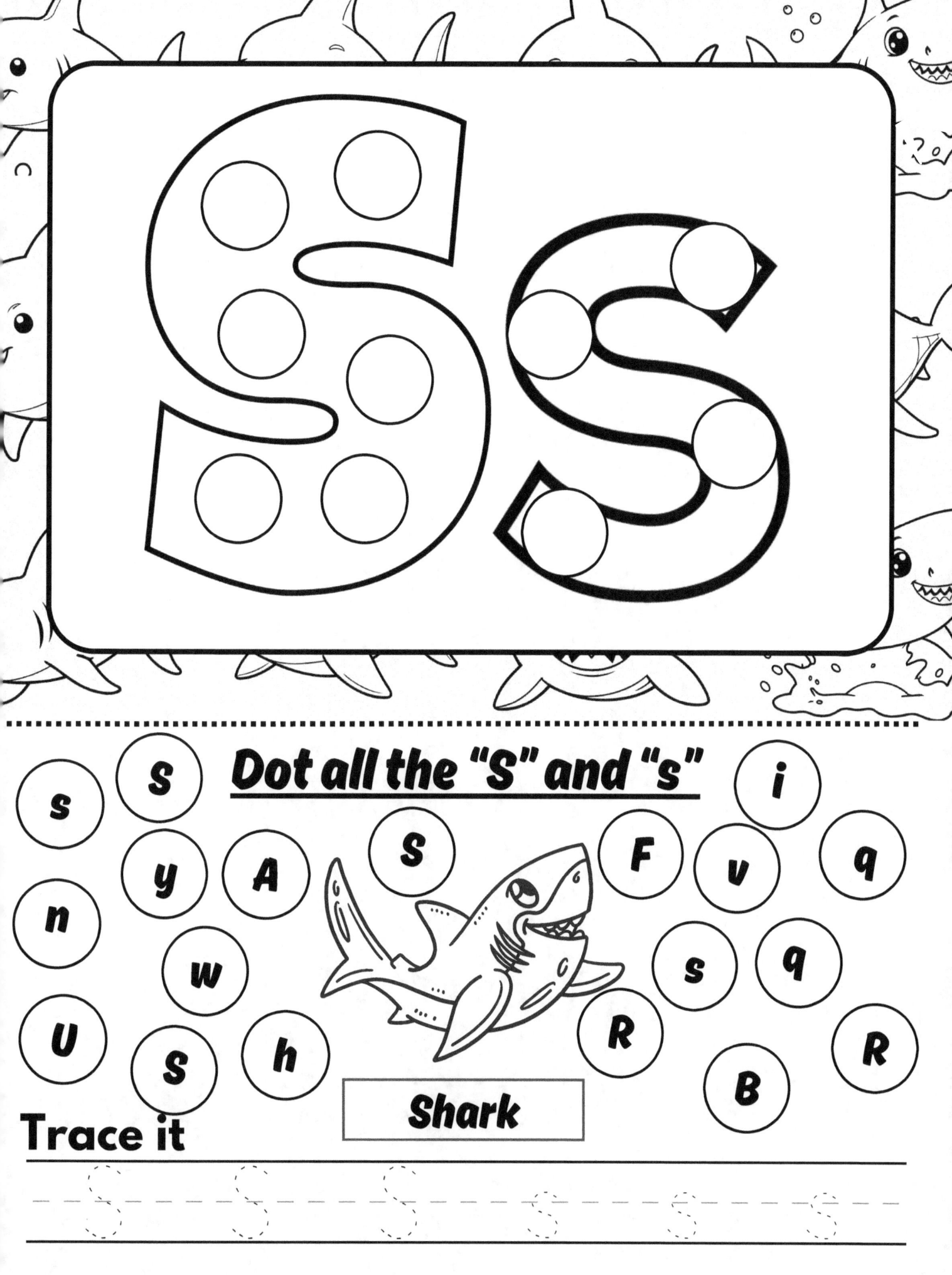

Dot all the "S" and "s"

Shark

Trace it

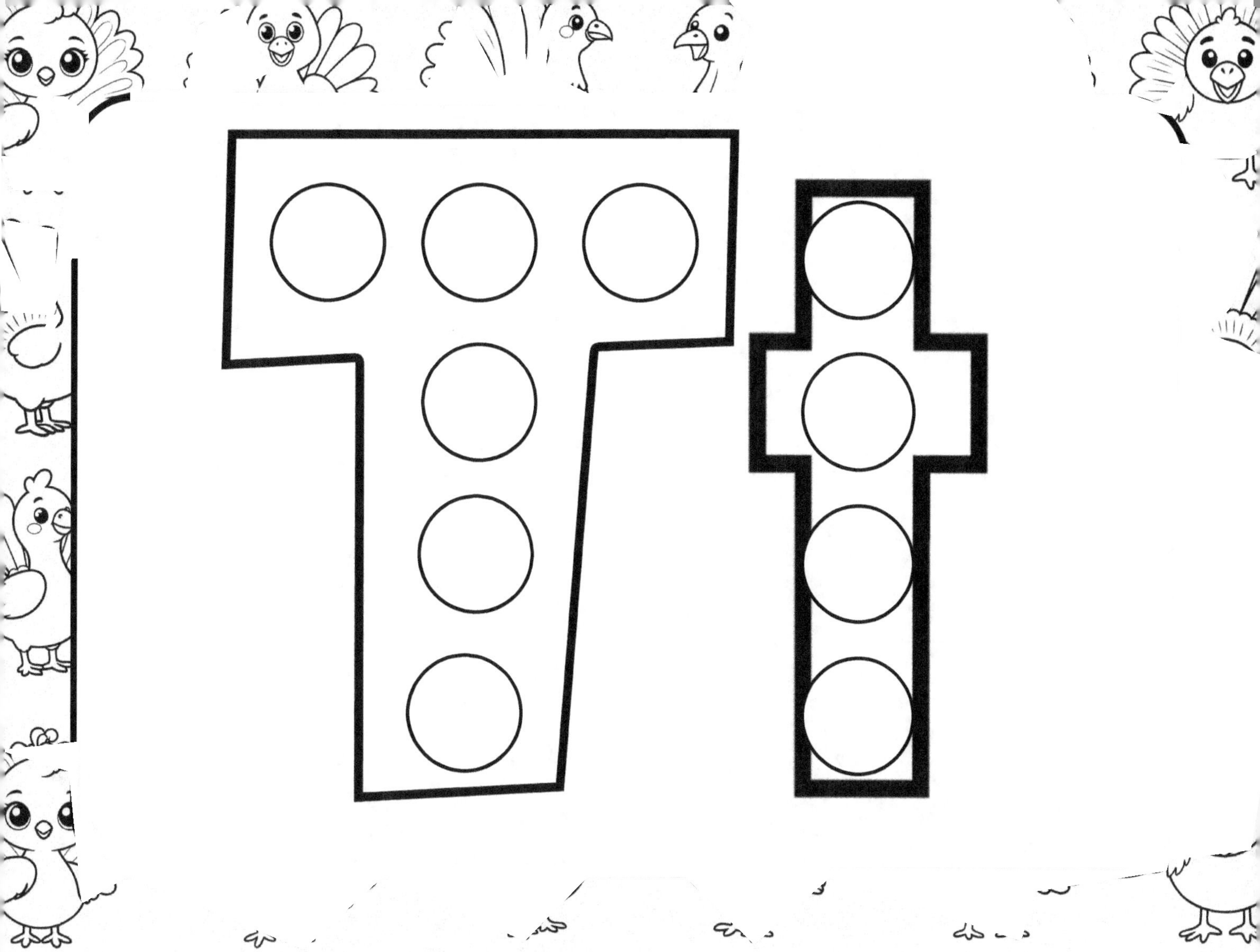

Dot all the "T" and "t"

s o t y A t d w T h

Turkey

t R F q T R S B

Trace it

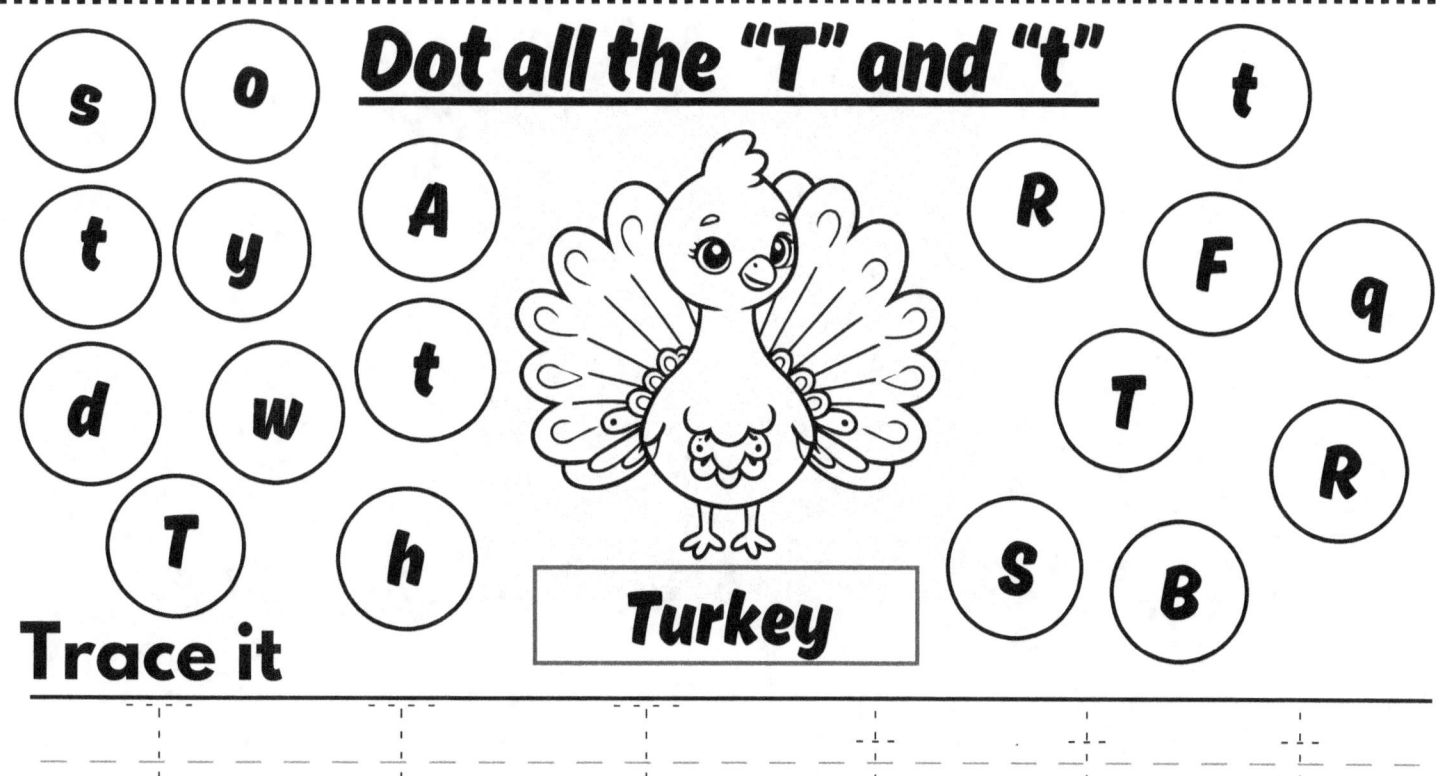

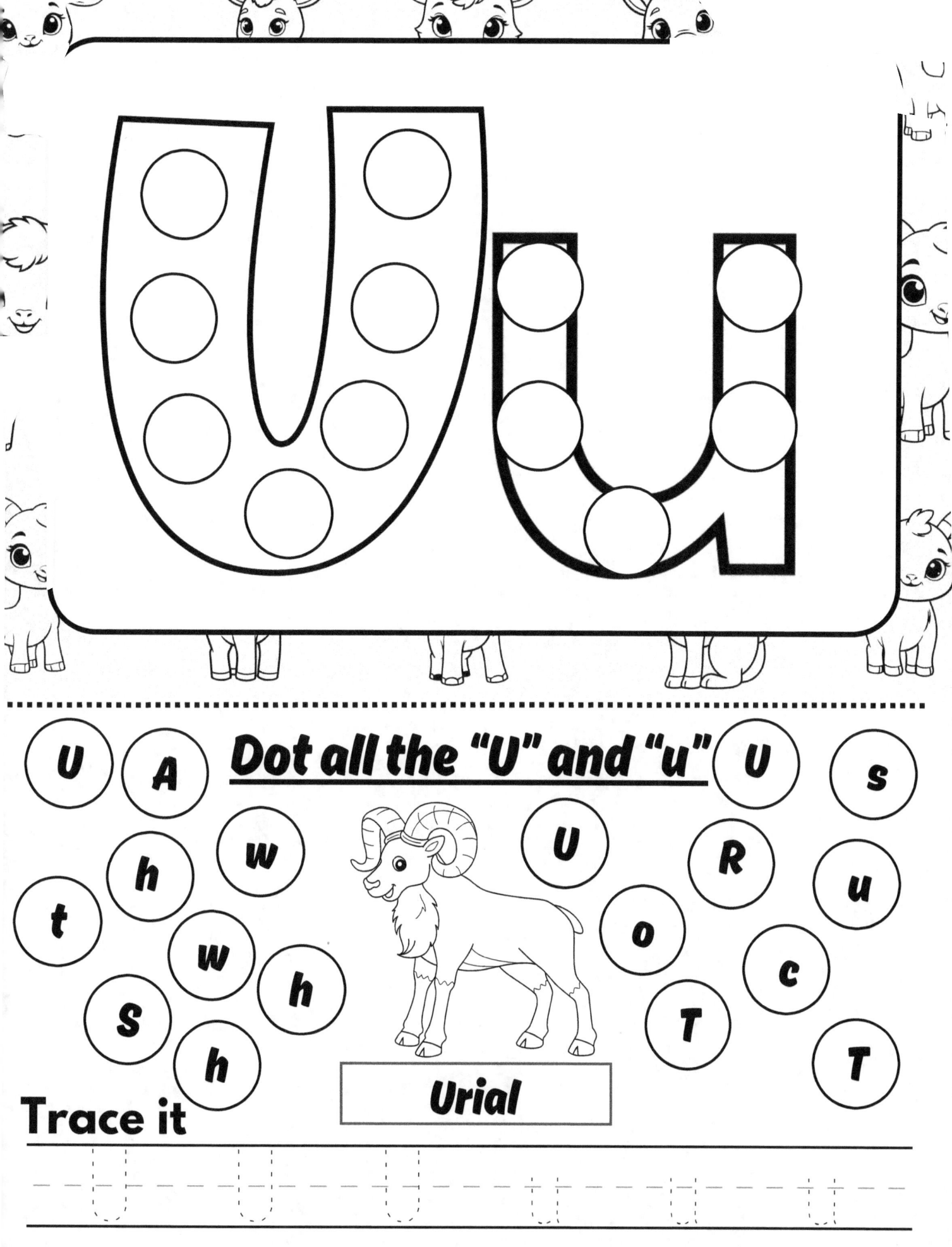

Dot all the "U" and "u"

U A

h

w

t

w

h

S

h

Urial

U s

U R u

o c

T T

Trace it

Dot all the "V" and "v"

Viper

Trace it

Dot all the "W" and "w"

f w R T

f w S A S y

S A S O w

W w s v W T

i E v L

Whale

Trace it

W   W   W   W   W   W

w   w   w   w   w   w

Dot all the "X" and "x"

Xerus

Trace it

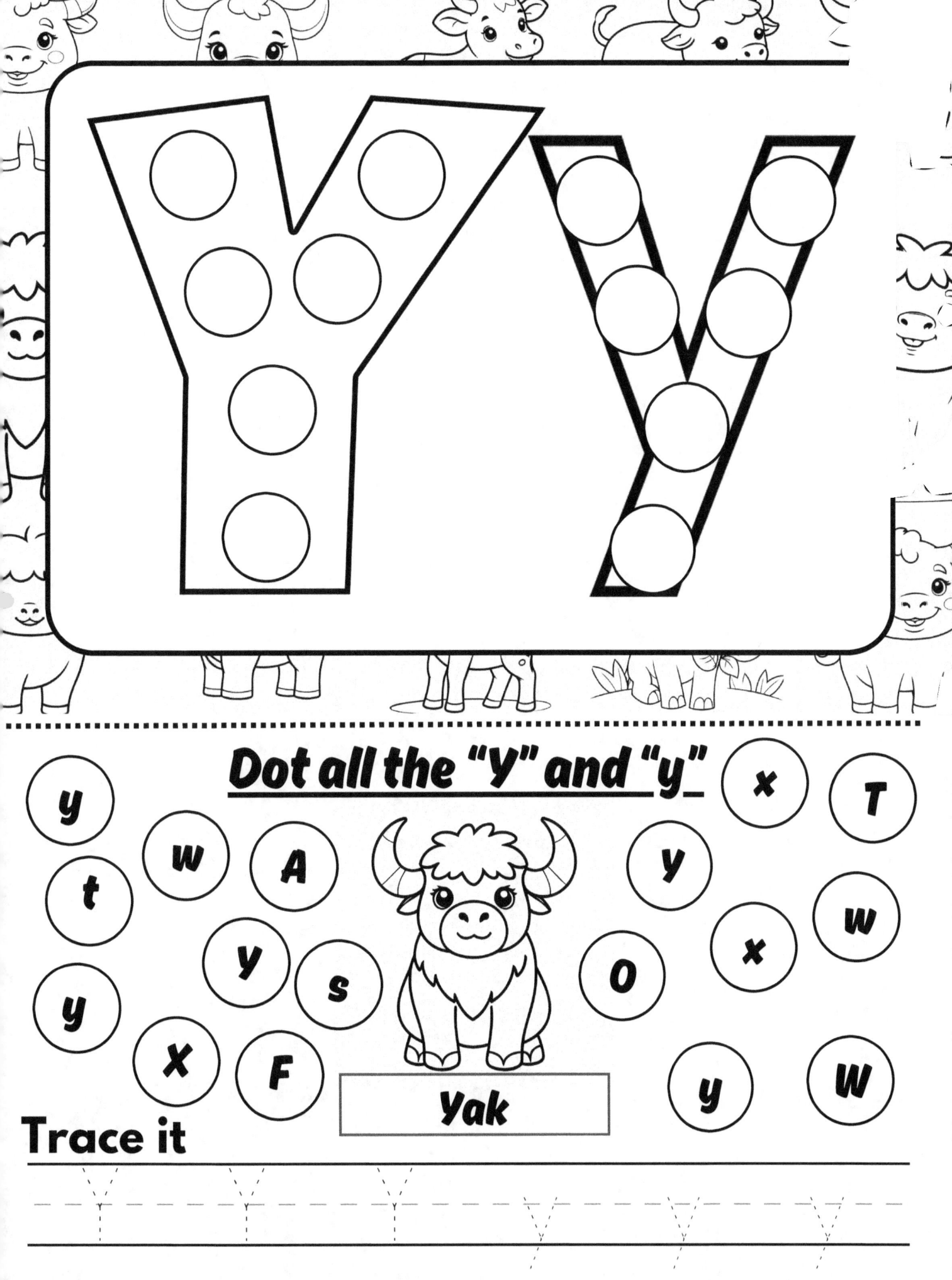

Dot all the "y" and "y"

y

y
t

w

A

y

y
s

X
F

Yak

x

T

y

x

W

O

x

W

y

W

Trace it

Dot all the "Z" and "z"

o c   z

t z   A   x   y   w

b F   G   O   y   Z

      X   Zebra   z

Trace it

0

2

6

1

8

5

8

0

1

0

5

9

Dot all the "O"

5

8

4

1

8

6

0

7

3

0

2

5

7

7

Trace it

0 0 0 0 0 0

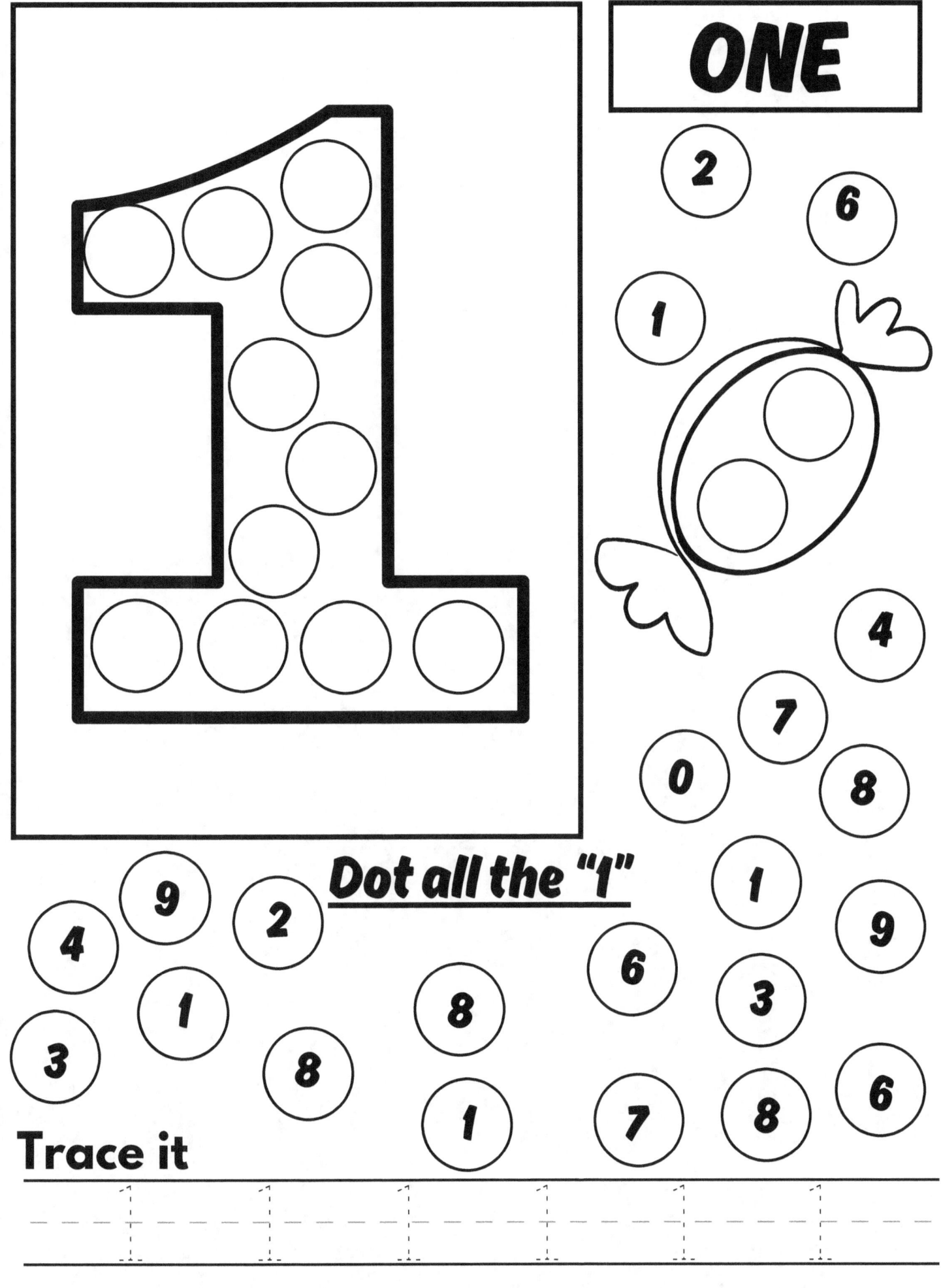

ONE

Dot all the "1"

Trace it

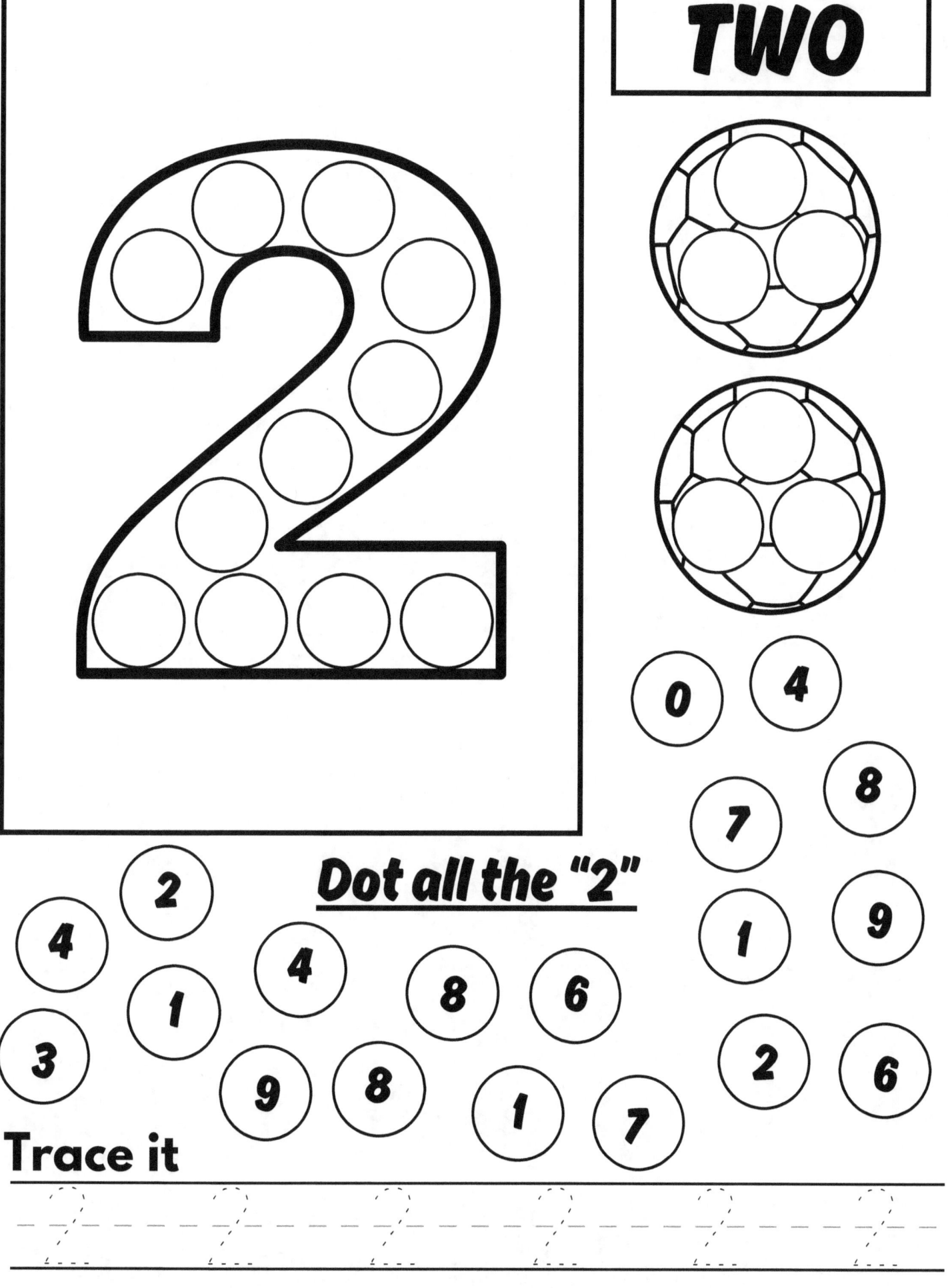

TWO

Dot all the "2"

Trace it

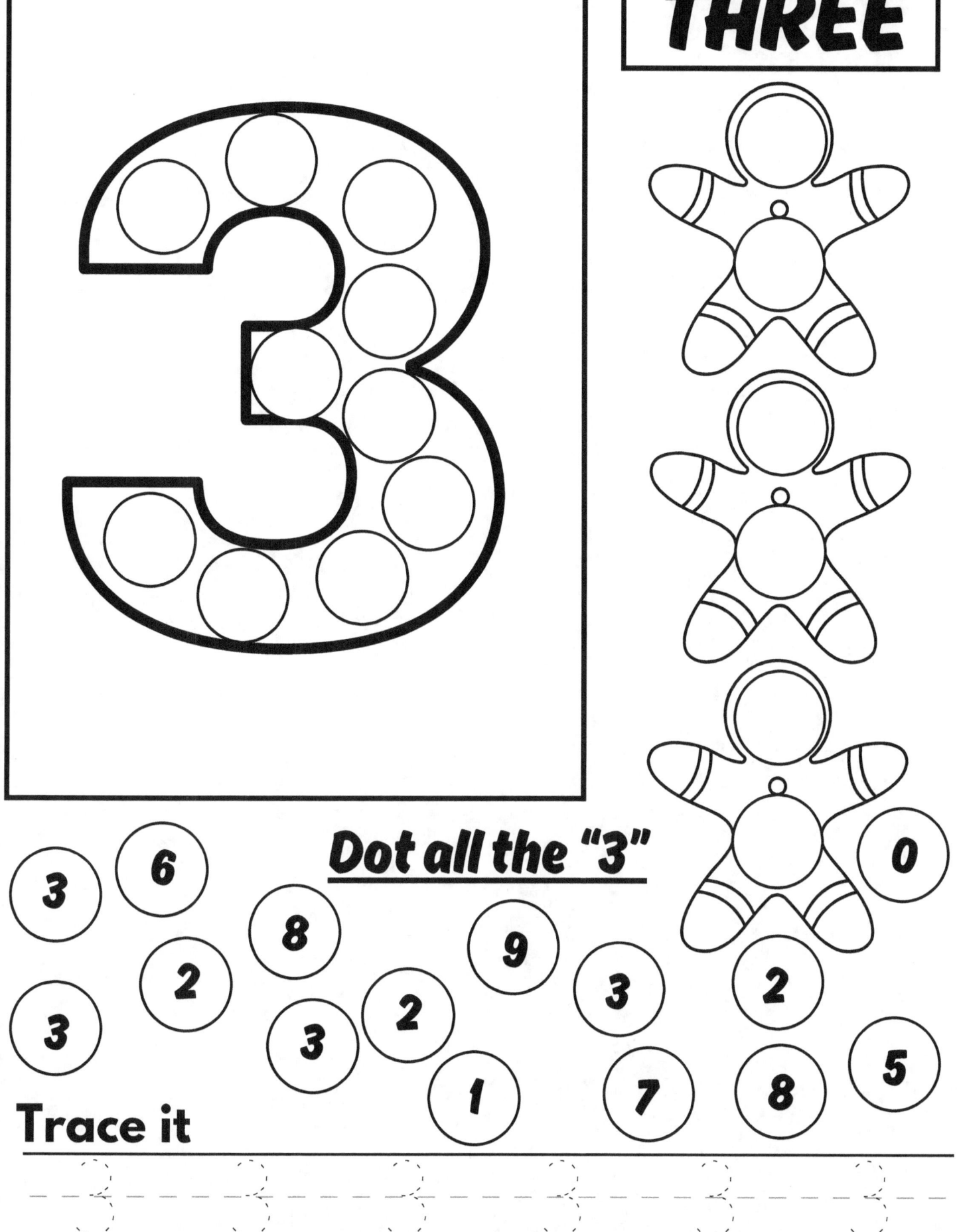

THREE

3

Dot all the "3"

3 6
8
2   9
2   3   2
3
3
1   7   8   5

0

Trace it

3 3 3 3 3 3

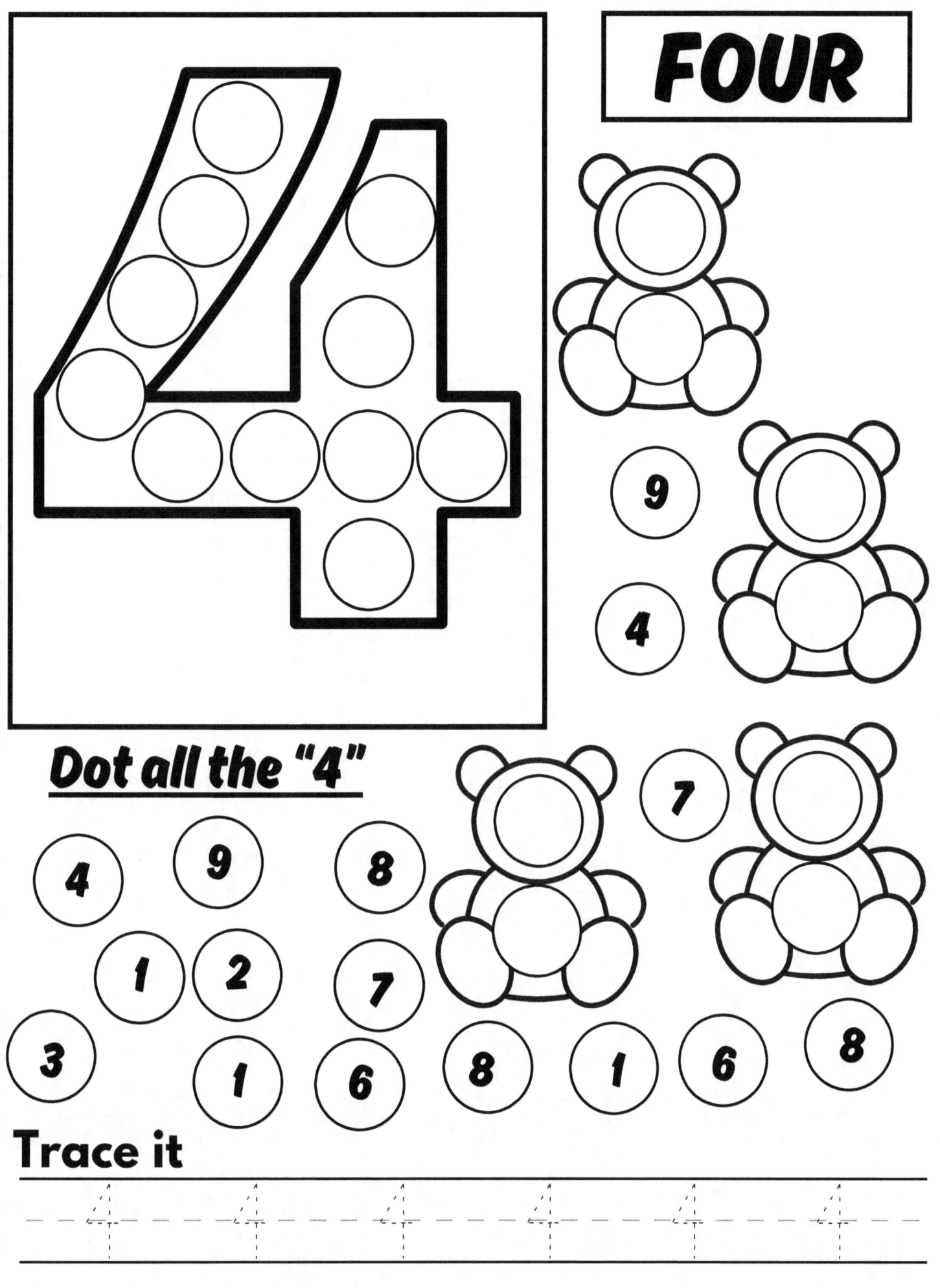

FOUR

Dot all the "4"

Trace it

FIVE

5

9

8

2

5

8

7

Dot all the "5"

4   6

5   9   1   5   7

4   4   8   6   7

Trace it

5 5 5 5 5 5 5

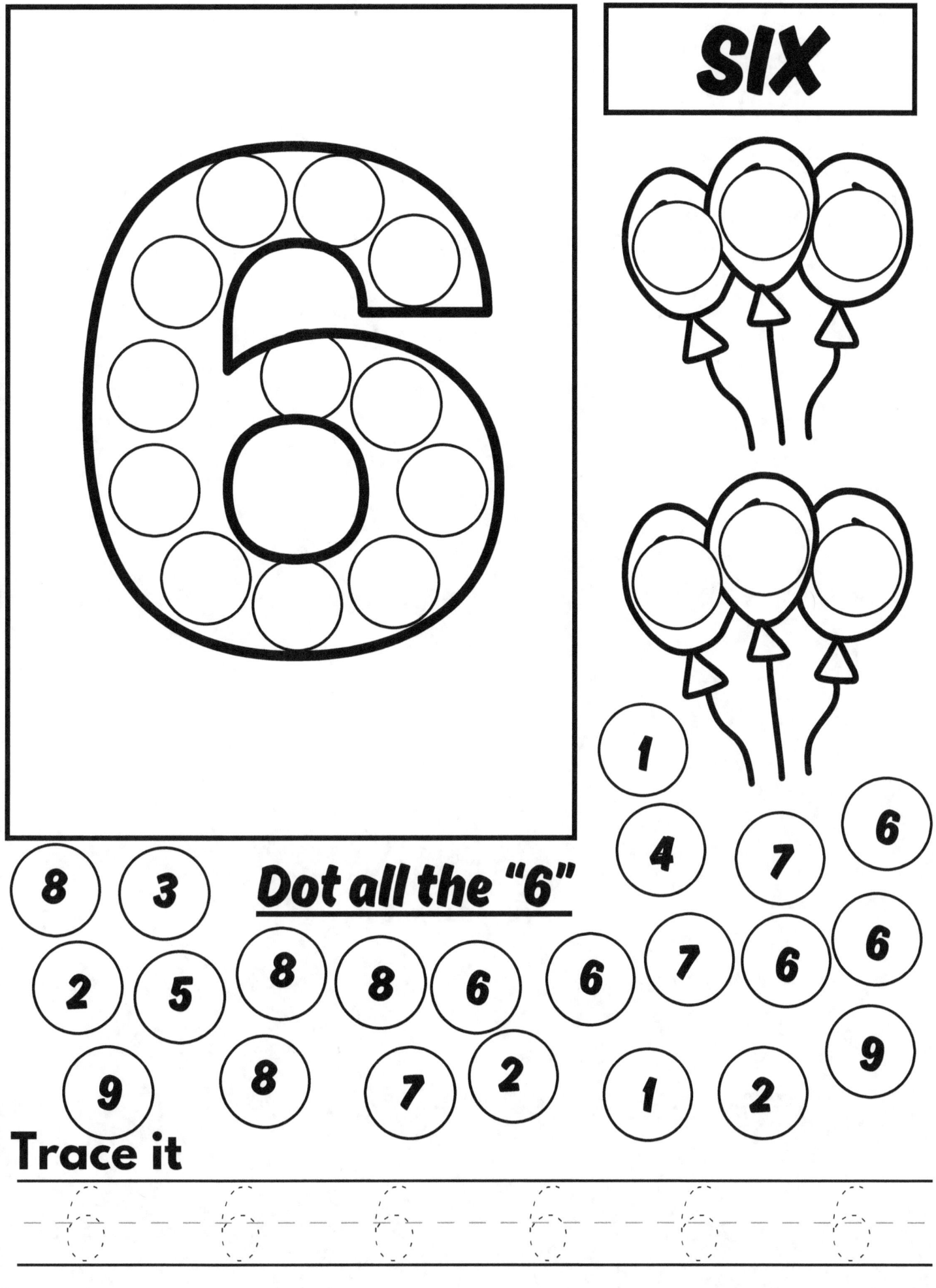

SIX

Dot all the "6"

Trace it

6 6 6 6 6 6

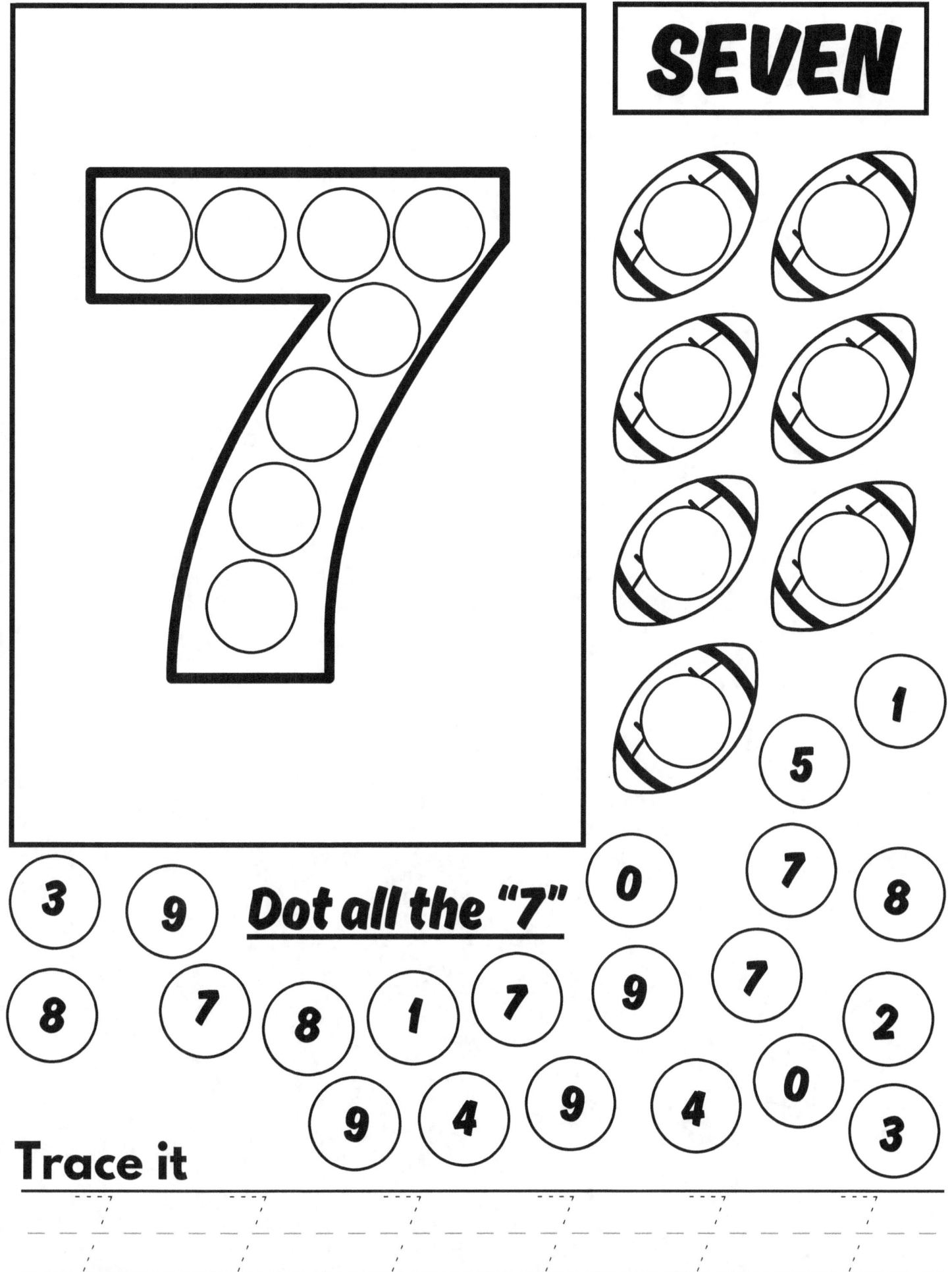

SEVEN

7

Dot all the "7"

3 9

8 7 8 1 7 9 7 8

9 4 9 4 0 2

1 5 0 7 4 0 3

Trace it

EIGHT

Dot all the "8"

4

1　5　4

8　　3　　8

9　4　　9　7　7　　8　6

1　　　1

Trace it

8　　8　　8　　8　　8

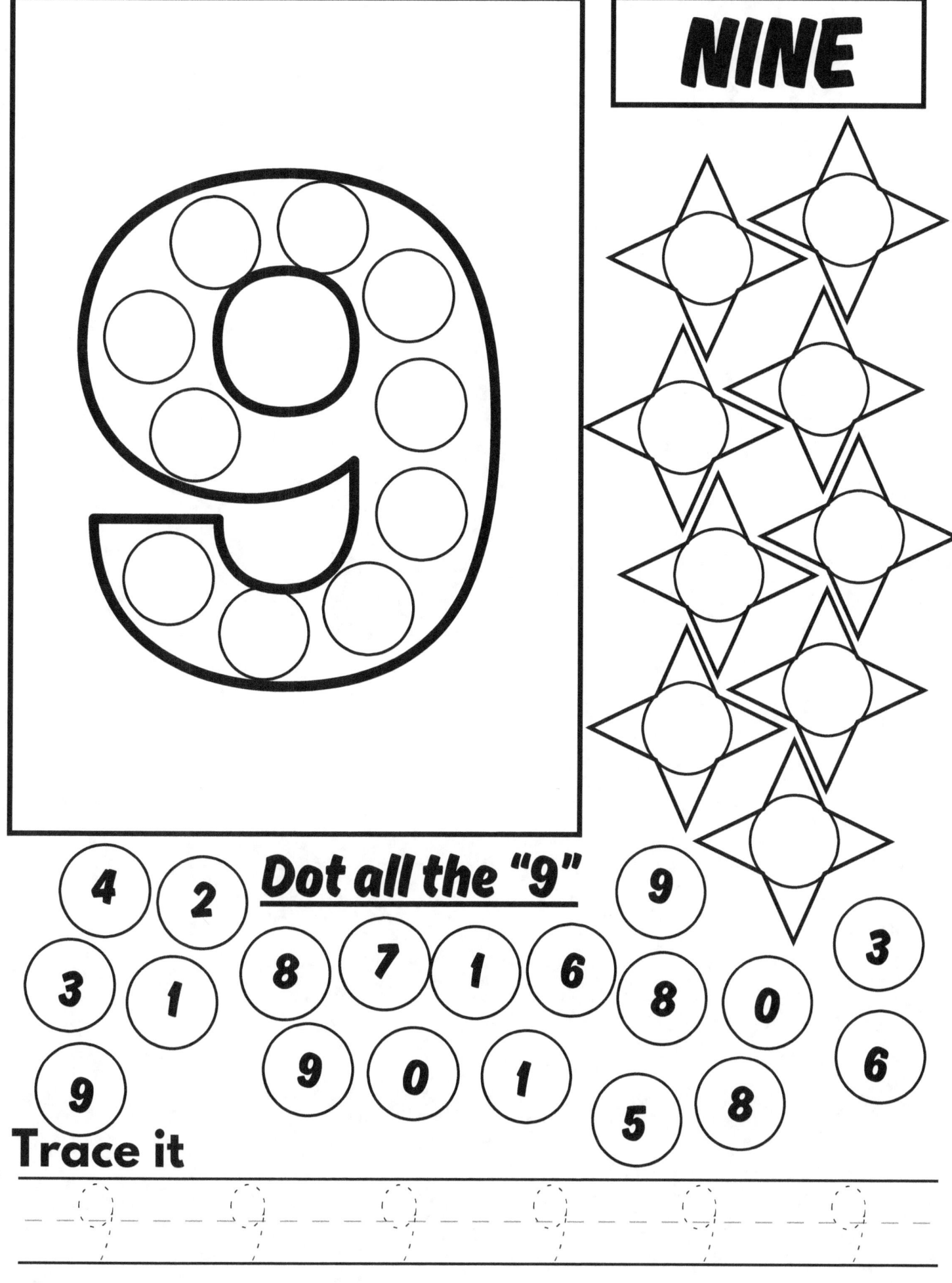

NINE

9

Dot all the "9"

4 2
3 1
9

8 7 1 6
9 0 1

9
8 0
5 8

3
6

Trace it

9 9 9 9 9 9

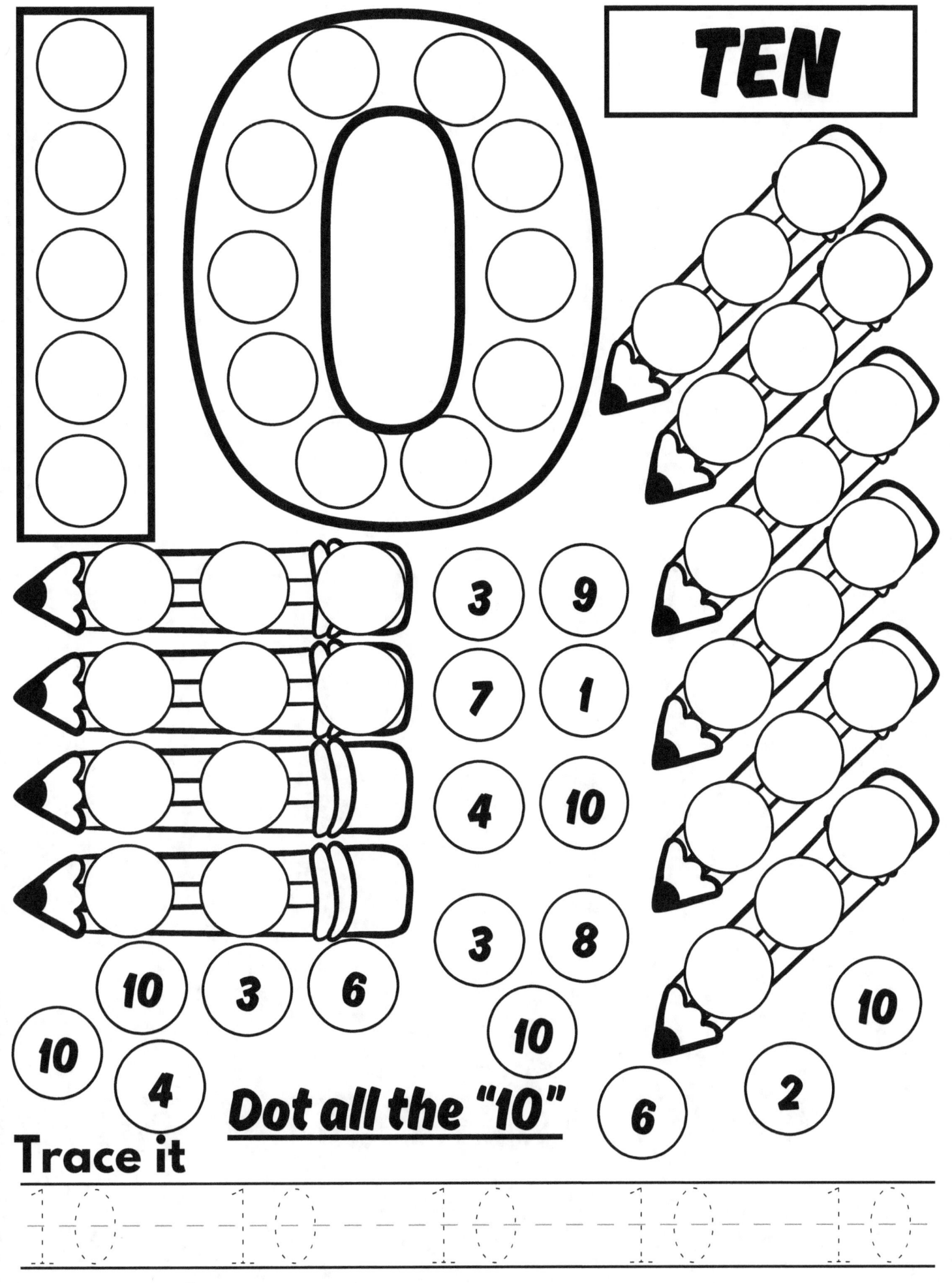

TEN

3 9
7 1
4 10
3 8
10 3 6
10
10
4
6 2 10

Dot all the "10"

Trace it

10   10   10   10   10

CIRCLE

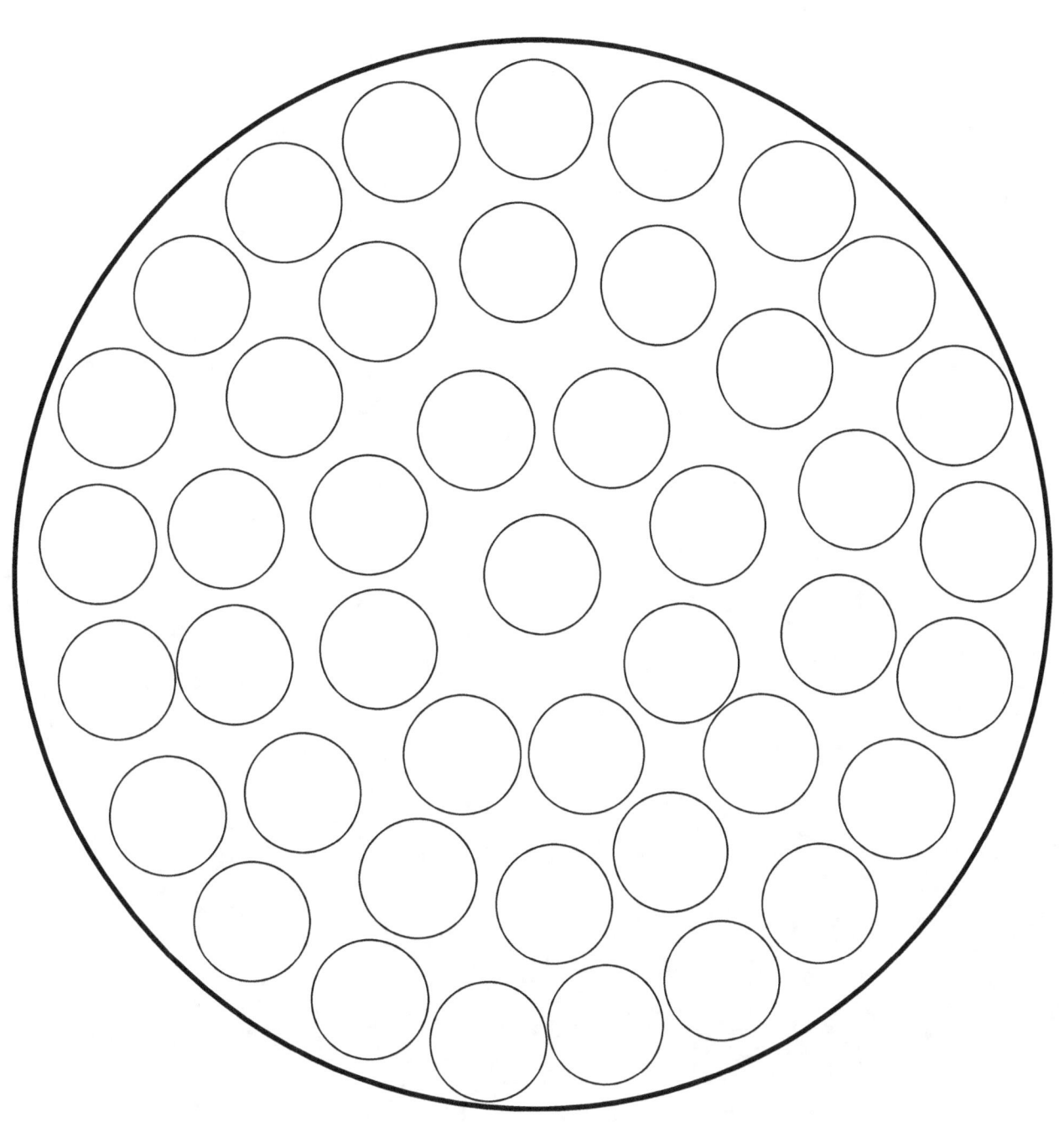

SQUARE

RECTANGLE

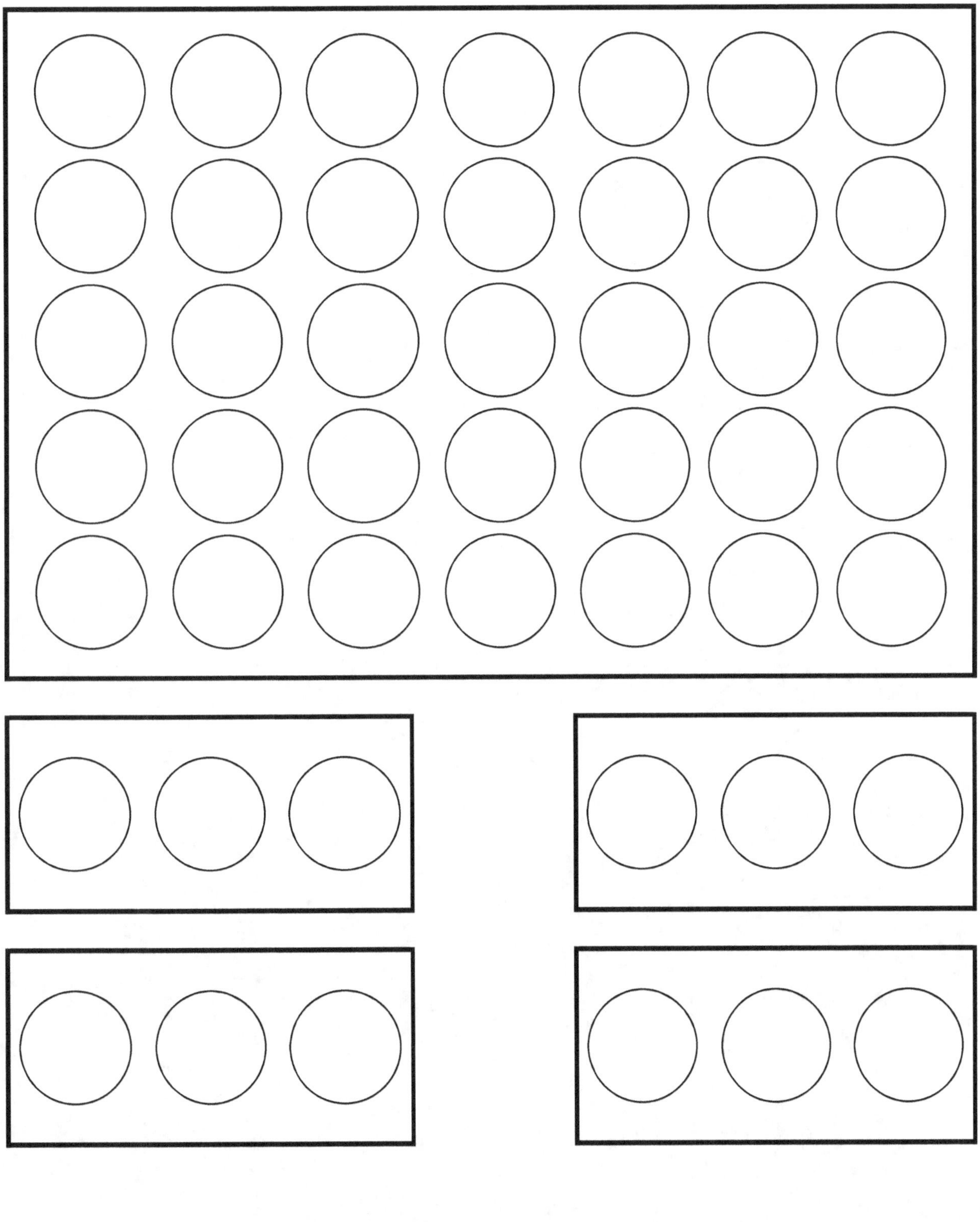

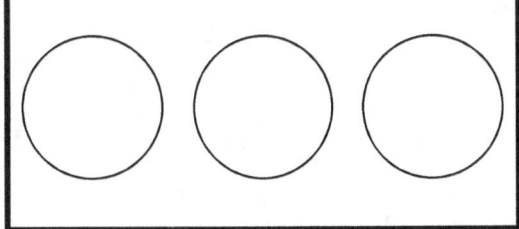
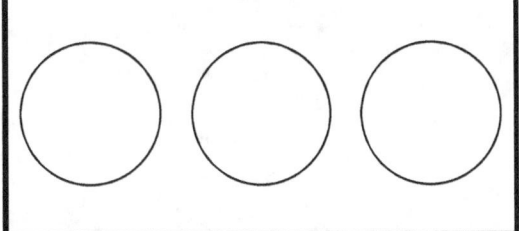
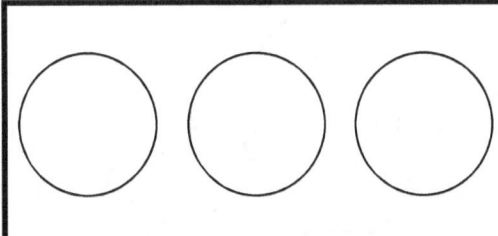
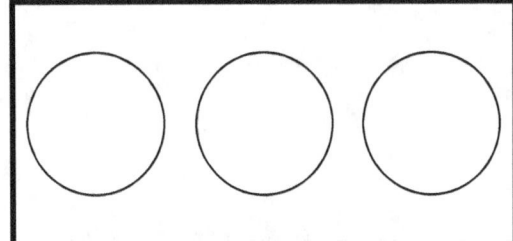

TRIANGLE

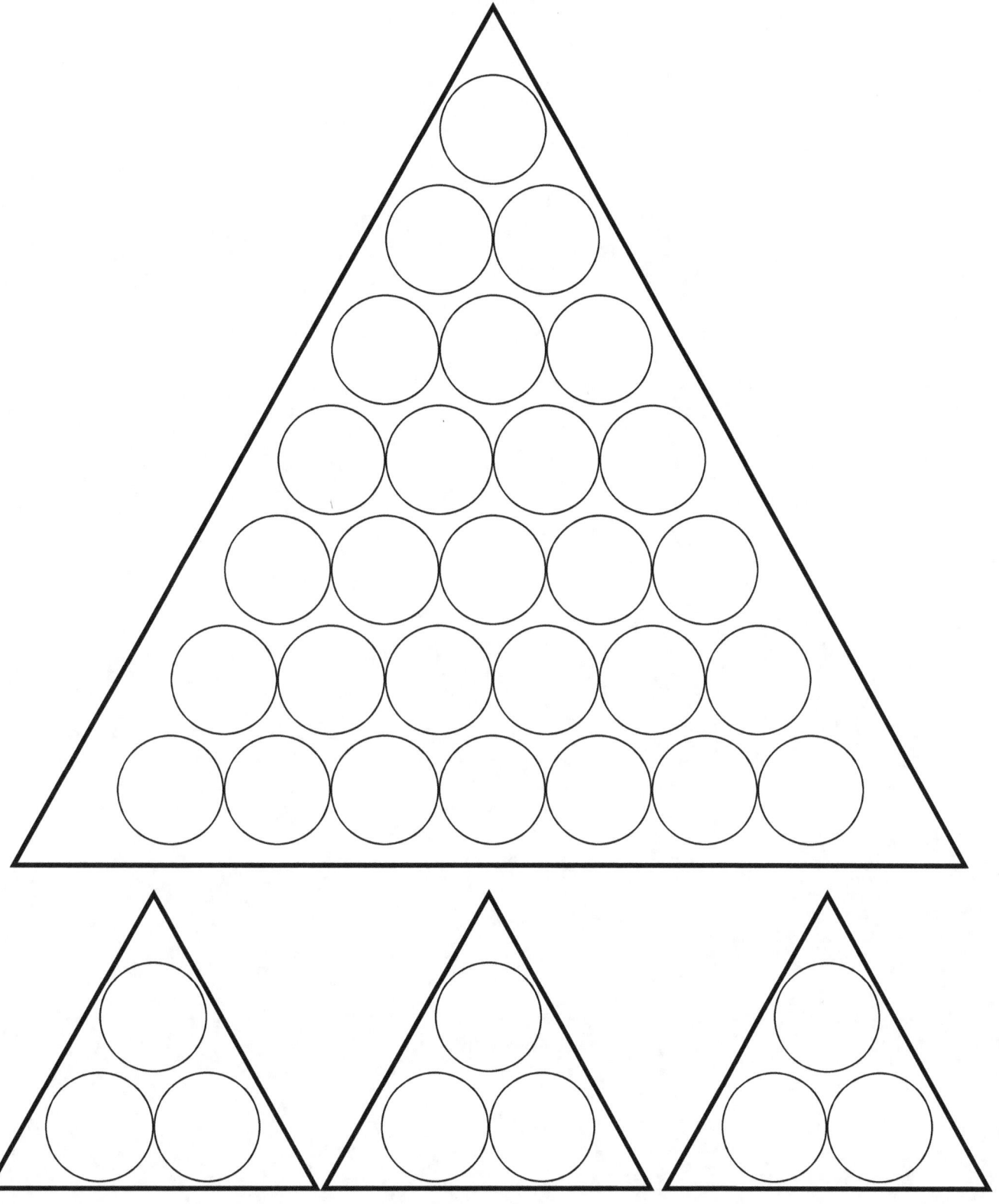

PENTAGON

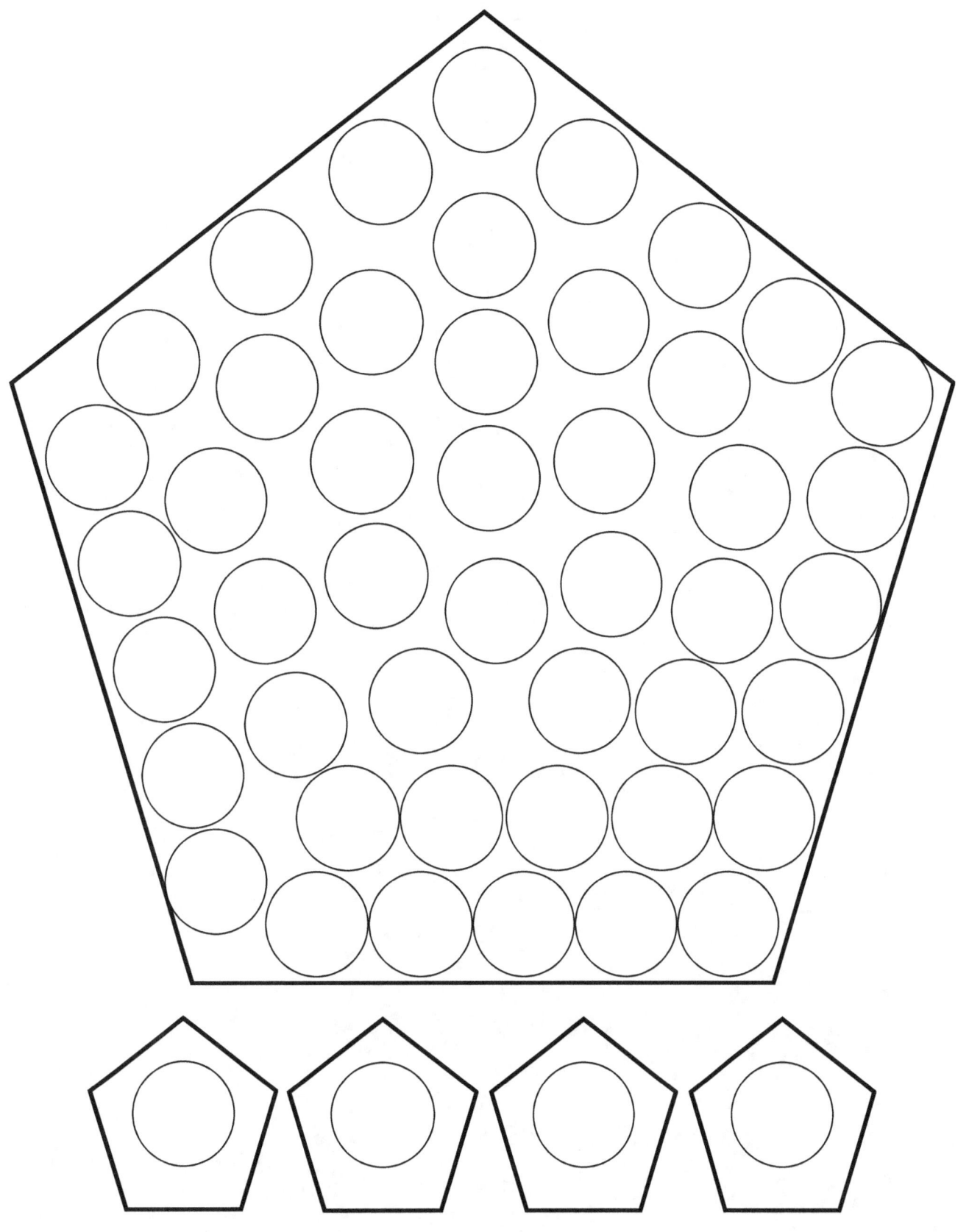

HEXAGON

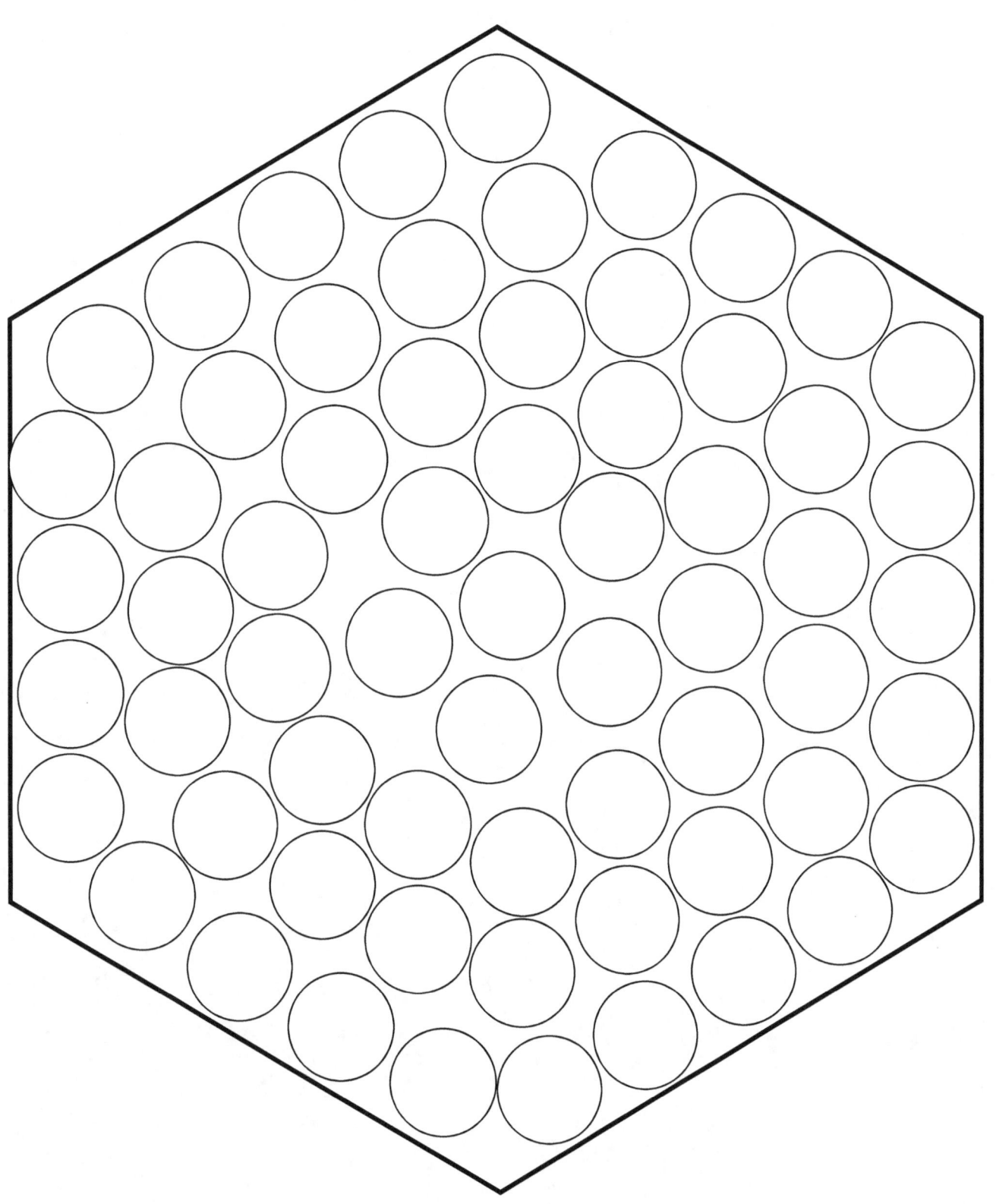

HEPTAGON

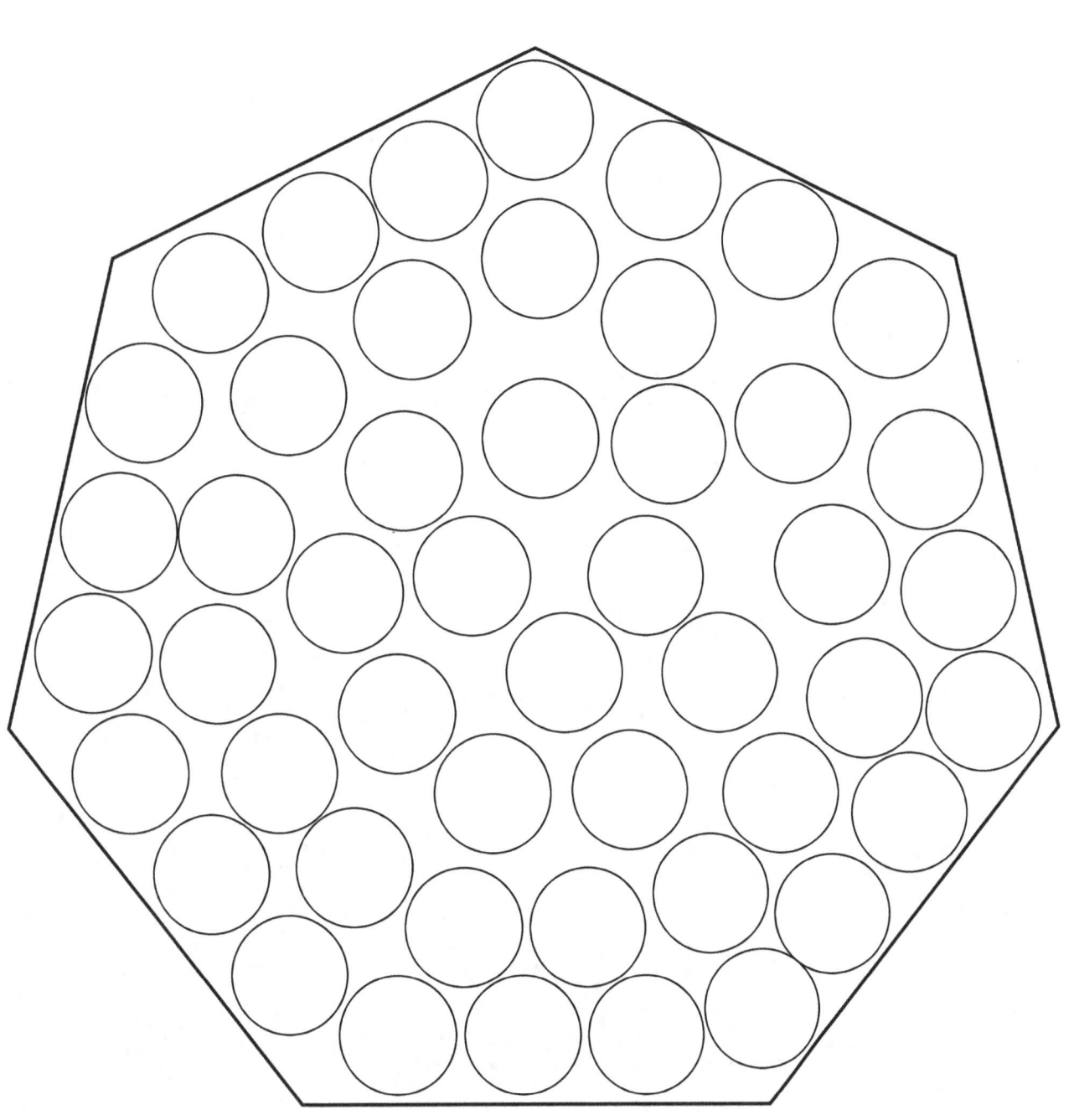

OCTAGON

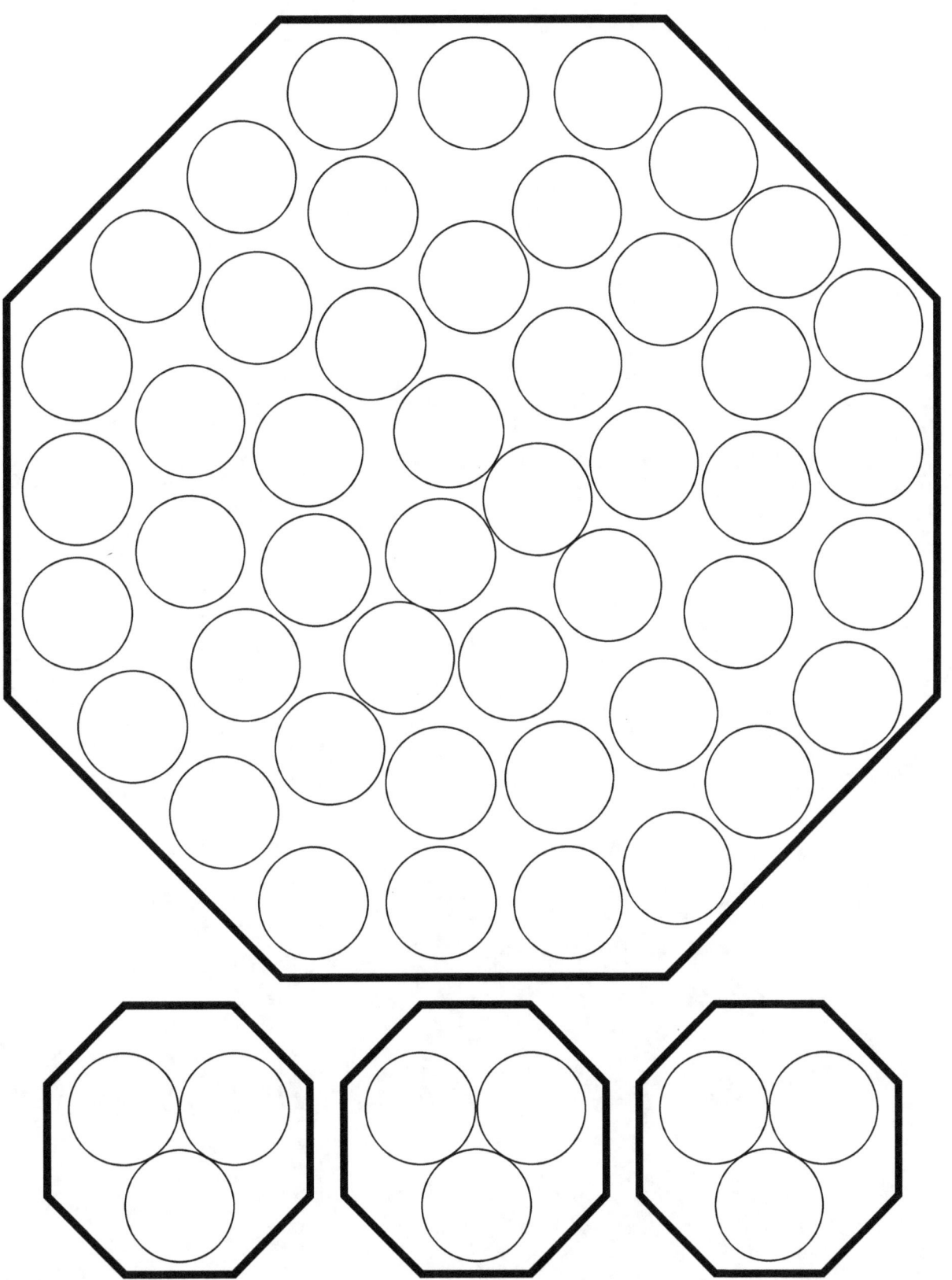

NONAGON

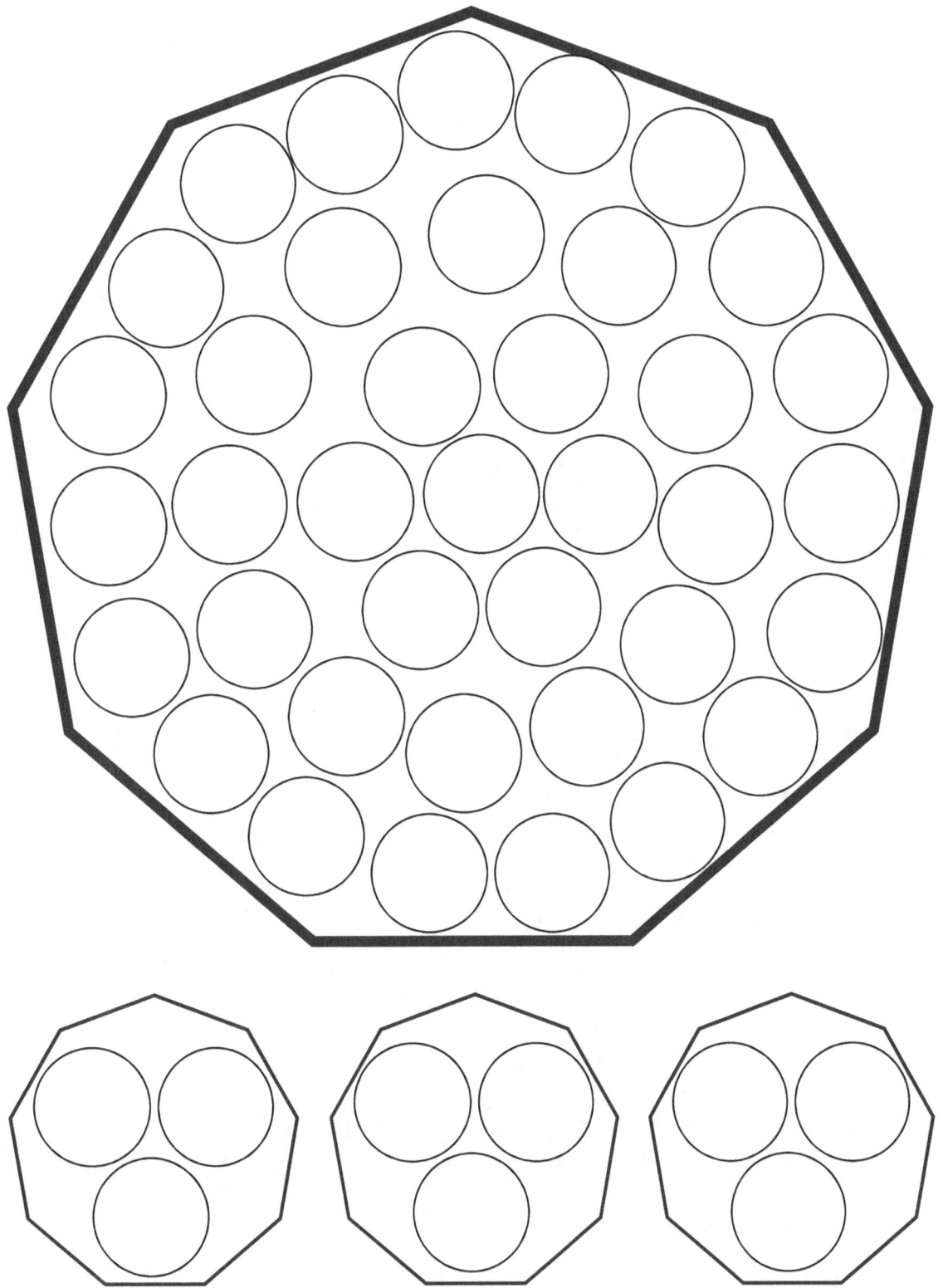

DECAGON

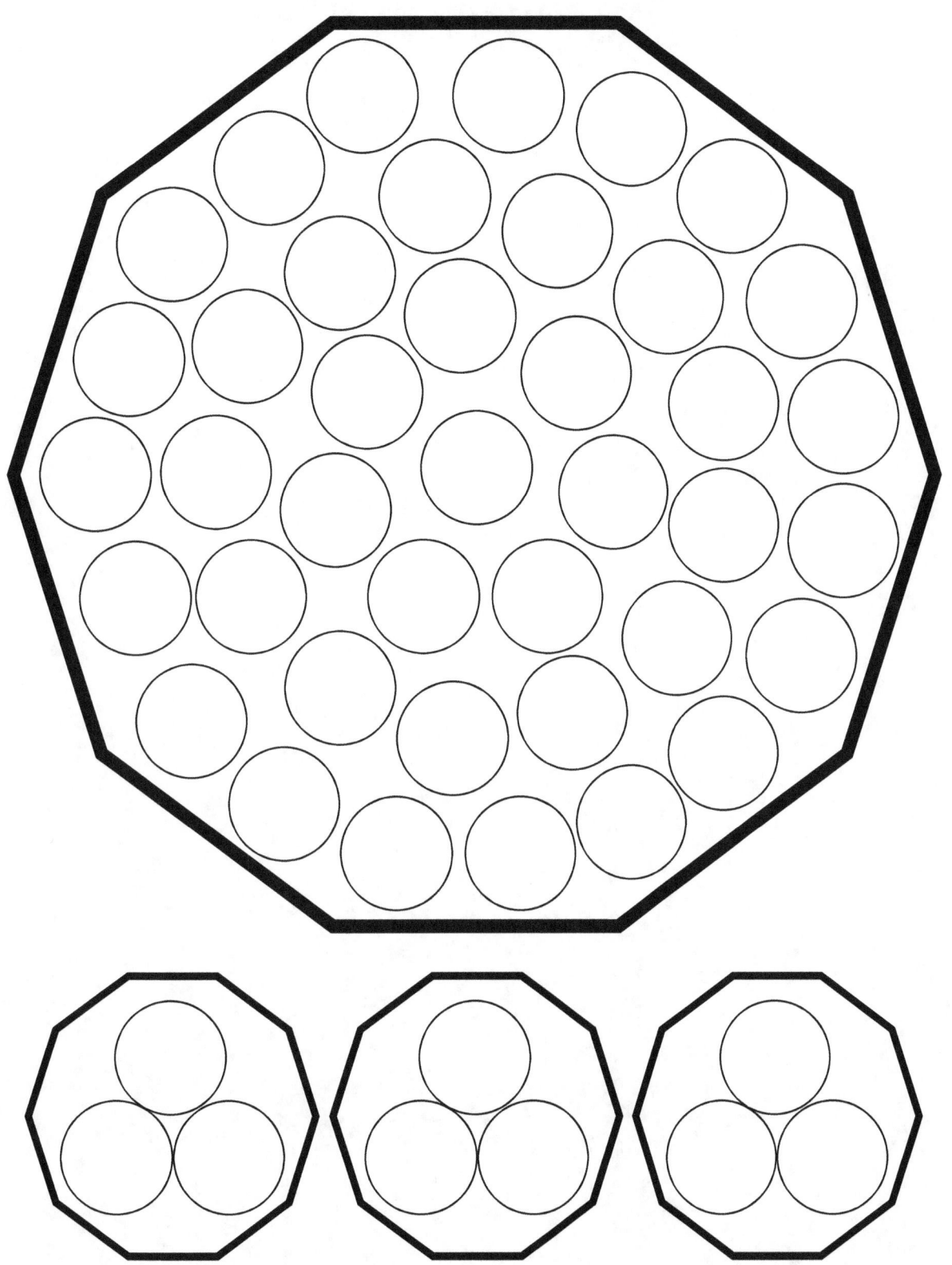

STAR

MOON

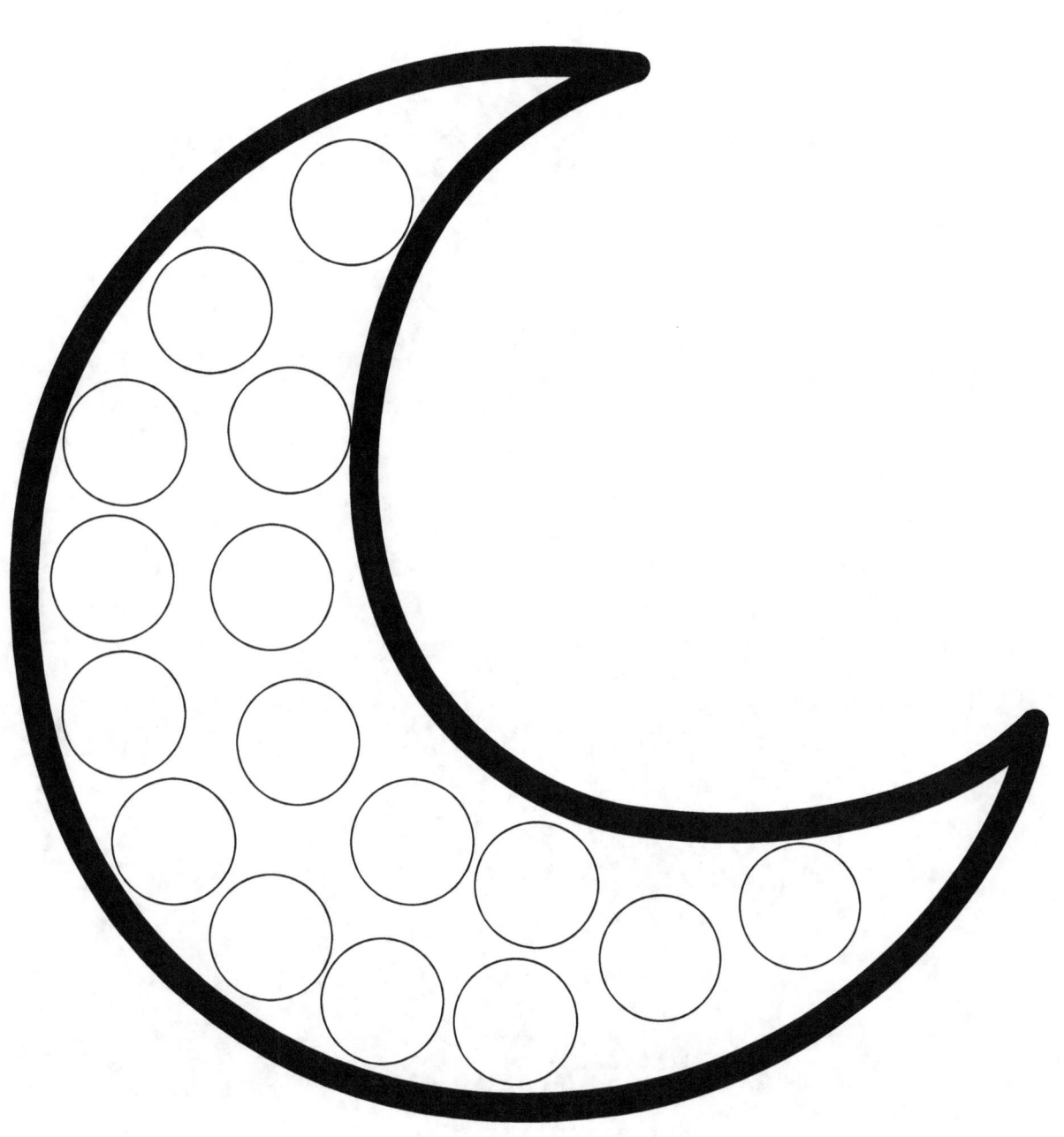

OVAL

HEART

CLOUD

Free Printable Activity Book!

- **Enhances Creativity:** Fun dot marker coloring pages.
- **Builds Fine Motor Skills:** Scissor skill exercises and dot-to-dot puzzles.
- **Boosts Cognitive Development:** Simple addition with numbers and images.
- **Encourages Observation:** Engaging I Spy games.
- **Hours of Fun:** Full kawaii coloring pages designed for young children.

SCAN ME

Parents & Teachers!

Our biggest joy comes from helping little ones flourish and discover the world around them through learning.

That's why your thoughts matter so much to us!

Your honest thoughts about our book, even a quick sentence or two, would mean the world. We really mean it!

You'd be making a big difference for a small education brand like ours, run with love by a mother-daughter team.

Your reviews help us reach more curious minds across the globe, paving their way to success in their educational journey.

And hey, maybe we'll even sell a few more books in the process!

Every single review makes our hearts swell with gratitude.

Ready to make our day?

Scan the QR Code below to share your thoughts.

www.ingramcontent.com/pod-product-compliance
Lightning Source LLC
Chambersburg PA
CBHW081004120626
46546CB00010B/3006